HATCHET JOBS

Also by Dale Peck

What We Lost
Now It's Time to Say Goodbye
The Law of Enclosures
Martin and John

HATCHET JOBS

Writings on
Contemporary Fiction

Dale Peck

THE NEW PRESS

NEW YORK
LONDON

Published in the United States by The New Press, New York, 2004
Distributed by W. W. Norton & Company, Inc., New York

Many of these pieces appeared, in slightly different form, in the
London Review of Books, The New Republic, and *The Village Voice.*

LIBRARY OF CONGRESS CATALOGING-IN-PUBLICATION DATA
Peck, Dale.
Hatchet jobs : writings on contemporary fiction / Dale Peck.
    p.   cm.
ISBN 1-56584-874-8
1. American literature—20th century—History and criticism.   I. Title.
PS225.P43 2004
810.9'005—dc22   2003070607

The New Press was established in 1990 as a not-for-profit alternative
to the large, commercial publishing houses currently dominating the book
publishing industry. The New Press operates in the public
interest rather than for private gain, and is committed to publishing, in
innovative ways, works of educational, cultural, and community value that
are often deemed insufficiently profitable.

The New Press
38 Greene Street, 4th floor
New York, NY 10013
www.thenewpress.com

In the United Kingdom:
6 Salem Road
London W2 4BU

Composition by dix!

Printed in the United States of America

2 4 6 8 10 9 7 5 3 1

This book is dedicated to Sally Singer,
who commissioned the first of its essays;
and her husband, Joe O'Neill,
who has been an indefatigable reader, good friend,
and introduced me to its publisher.

I owe an extra-special thank you to Jim Lewis, who knew
everything I know about fiction before I did.
I apologize if I got it all wrong.

All I said was:
there, you see, it is broken
—WILLIAM CARLOS WILLIAMS, *Spring and All*

Contents

HATCHET JOBS

Big Brother Is Calling You Names

In July 2002, I raised a ruckus in the publishing world when I panned Rick Moody's memoir *The Black Veil* at some length in the *New Republic*. Let me be honest: my review was scathing. *Salon* described it as "an author's darkest nightmare," as if writers spend time dreaming of what critics will say about us. Well, we probably do, and any piece that begins "So-and-so is the worst writer of his generation" probably isn't going to brighten the nights of the author in question—or his publisher, agent, friends, or fans.

Cocktail party gossip soon yielded pieces in *New York* magazine and the *Observer*, online at *Salon* and Plastic.com and at least a dozen blogs. Most of the commentary denounced me, not so much for what I'd written as for the vehemence with which I'd phrased it. The backlash reached its nadir in March 2003, in a massive essay Heidi Julavits wrote for the debut issue of *The Believer*. In the piece, which serves as a manifesto for the new magazine, Julavits called for a literary culture that supports "experimentation" and "ambition" in general, and, more

specifically, resists the urge to indulge in "snarky" book reviewing. The fact that *The Believer* is the latest venture from the
publisher of *McSweeney's* magazine and McSweeney's Books,
Dave Eggers, and that most of the negatively reviewed writers
Julavits mentions—Rick Moody, Marc Nesbitt, Zadie Smith—
are associated with both the magazine and the "aesthetic tradition" it promotes, seemed to raise very few eyebrows. Rather,
Julavits was said to have "draw[n] a line in the sand against the
unbelievers." I suspect, then, that it will please Julavits (if not
Moody himself) to know that this author, at least, has decided
to follow her advice. *Hatchet Jobs* marks my final foray into negative book reviewing. As soon as I finish this introduction, I am
throwing away my red pen. I will no longer write negative
book reviews.

Hatchet jobs are nothing new, particularly when one novelist goes after another. The "disinterested" book critic is a relatively recent invention. Before that there were academics and
there were writers—poets, essayists, playwrights, novelists. If
you considered yourself a serious practitioner of any genre, you
were expected to weigh in on the aesthetic concerns of the day.
Objectivity wasn't the point: passion was. Coleridge wrote
adoringly of his friend Wordsworth in both verse and prose,
while Poe wrote adoringly of himself in "The Philosophy of
Composition." When James Joyce's *Ulysses* began appearing in
magazine installments, Virginia Woolf pronounced him the
"notable" writer of her generation. "Mr. Joyce," she wrote, "is
spiritual."

But after the full text of the novel had been published she
revised her opinion downward. "*Ulysses* was a memorable catastrophe—immense in daring, terrific in disaster." In her jour-

nals she was less tactful, declaring the book "diffuse," "brack-ish," "pretentious," and "underbred." The journals were even-tually published, and it's the zingers that stuck. Though even a cursory reading of Woolf reveals that she and Joyce were, sty-listically, closer than any of the other Modernists, it is in the anecdotal rather than aesthetic realm that most readers—in-cluding readers who are writers—choose to remember their relationship. Mud-slinging is just more fun to read than a dis-cussion of how stream-of-consciousness narration renders synaptic processes in prose.

So much for history. The scope of the reaction to my Moody essay pleased me at first. It also surprised me. Since 1996 I'd been registering my dissatisfaction with contempo-rary fiction in a series of reviews panning the work of everyone from Stanley Crouch to David Foster Wallace to Julian Barnes, with little more than the occasional email from a friend to reg-ister my efforts. But my pleasure faded as I realized that people were less interested in what I (or the writers I'd reviewed) had to say than in the possibility of a brawl. Like schoolboys chant-ing "Fight, fight," they let loose their own ripostes: I was "a troubled queen," according to one commentator. My reviews "degrade the profession," said another. I was "foolish," "bitchy" and finally "snarky."

God knows the name-calling doesn't bother me (although you'd think a clever writer wouldn't have to resort to homo-phobia to defend his novel). But it does effectively destroy my ability to be read seriously, by which I mean holistically. I'm the *New Republic* writer who called Rick Moody the worst writer of his generation, and the thousands of words I used to qualify that assertion have disappeared behind it. It took decades for

Woolf's opinion of Joyce to be reduced to a few catch-phrases, but only a few weeks for the 5,700 words of my review of *The Black Veil* to be boiled down to its first sentence, and about the same time for the 9,200 words of Julavits' essay to be reduced to a single adjective. I would think Julavits might be bothered by such a development, but apparently not: in its July 2003 issue, *The Believer* announced "Snarkwatch," a forum for readers to record "disgruntled reactions to 'critical activity,' " an Orwellian call for denouncers that would seem Stalinesque if it weren't more reminiscent of schoolyard snitching. One of its first contributors? None other than Rick Moody.

As uninteresting (if slightly reprehensible) as "Snark-watch" may be, it does help unmask the agenda of the essay which engendered it. There, Julavits singled out several reviews for snarkiness (including my Moody piece, Sam Sifton's review of Marc Nesbitt's *Gigantic*, James Wood's review of Zadie Smith's *The Autograph Man*, and Colson Whitehead's review of Richard Ford's *A Multitude of Sins*) but failed to quote from any of them at great length in order to illustrate how we hadn't "tr[ied] to understand . . . what a certain book is trying to do." In fact the only piece she quoted from at all was Sifton's. The tacit assumption here is that everyone knows what snark is, and perhaps everyone does. But what is snark *not?* At what point does "criticism" turn into "screed"? For example, in Wood's review of *The Autograph Man*, is it the line *"White Teeth*, for all its many miracles, occasionally revealed a cartoonish energy" that bears traces of what Julavits calls a "hostile, knowing, bitter tone of contempt"? Or: "Such vacancy is embedded deep in the texture of the prose"? Or: "It is like reading a newspaper designed by a kindergarten. (Or by the editorial staff of *McSweeney's*.)"? Julavits declines direct comment, writing instead, "Wood famously abhors the aesthetic tradition in which Smith works. Rather than overcompensating for his known bias (a potentially interesting tack) or surprising us by delivering the last verdict we'd expect, he made a savage dive for the jugular."

Julavits is suggesting two things here: first, that it would have been more "interesting" for Wood to pretend to like *The Autograph Man* than to say what he really feels, and second, that it is wrong—a "bias," "a mistake"—for one of the most respected literary critics in England and America to write about a tradition he doesn't merely "abhor," but would like to see the end of. What Julavits is implying, finally, is that critics who don't believe, as she does, that a book is "ambitious" or even "literary" must be lying. The idea that their "hostility" and "contempt" might reflect an "admirable passion" for literature (as Joe Hagan suggested in the *Observer*) is never allowed for. Rather, she calls into question their motivations ("self-serving and mean," "anti-intellectual") and their methods ("disdainful," "clichéd disparagements"). She labels them "bitchy," knowing that it is no more useful to counter such an allegation with protestations that one's beliefs are just as "strongly-held" as hers than it is to deny allegations of spousal abuse by saying that you no longer beat your wife.

Perhaps this last is the most disturbing, or simply duplicitous, aspect of Ms. Julavits' essay. "Reading many reviews these days . . . I have the feeling of dust settling on a razed landscape, in which nothing is growing, in which nothing can grow." Such a sentiment seems slightly out of place in the context of Richard Ford, Rick Moody, Salman Rushdie, Zadie Smith, and David Foster Wallace—not to mention Ms. Julavits and Mr. Eggers—who all earn millions of dollars by selling many,

many copies of their work. But to the degree that their massive literary advances and domination of display and review space have crowded out competitors, it seems fair to say that the writers who *can* legitimately claim to be working in a literary "wasteland" are those whose ambitions, intellect, and experiments are neither "mainstream" nor in sync with her own, her employer's, and his publishing ventures. Ms. Julavits isn't trying to foster anything. She's trying to hold on to her slice of the pie, whether you define that in financial or aesthetic terms.

Seven years ago I wrote about the trap of praise that had engulfed Kurt Vonnegut, effectively silencing him as a critic of his times. At the time I hadn't realized that the inverse is also true: that labels attach themselves not to words or books (or book reviews) but to writers, and that once you've been labeled a certain kind of writer—in my case foolish, troubled, snarky, etc.—readers will approach anything you write looking for (and finding) evidence of precisely those traits. I suppose it could be argued that reminiscence simplifies everything: in his original review of *Ulysses*, Edmund Wilson wrote, "There must be something wrong with a design which involves so much that is dull," before concluding that Joyce's novel was a work of "high genius" compared to which "the texture of other novelists seems intolerably loose." We remember the gist of things rather than the cavils, Wilson's "genius," Woolf's "catastrophe." People who shop at Barnes and Noble voted *Ulysses* the best novel of the last century, and who's to tell them different? There was a point when I would have liked to, but apparently that's just because I'm a bitch.

1

The Man Who Would Be Sven

My Sky Blue Trades by Sven Birkerts

1. It's like rain on your wedding day . . .

Here's criticism's trade secret: you can find meaning in anything if you look hard enough. Contemplate a work of art and patterns inevitably emerge, echoes, resonances, allusions which can be brought out and amplified through exegesis, the interpretive conceit by which a critic simultaneously deconstructs and rebuilds, unveils and augments another writer's metaphors, another writer's vision. Part attention to detail, part science, part Vulcan mind meld, exegesis allows a critic to enter and extend the context of a work of art, whether it be through the useful reductions of Sunday book reviews, the half millennium of minutiae that have accumulated to make Shakespeare "The Bard," or revelatory reappraisals in the manner of D.H. Lawrence's resuscitation of the writing of Herman Melville.

It's the latter efforts that tend to capture our attention, but it's important to remember at the outset that exegesis is only incidentally or latterly concerned with aesthetic quality. Its uncritical methodology can no more tell the difference between *Hollywood Wives* and *The Iliad* than a microscope's lens can, on its own, distinguish between a drop of Jackie Collins' blood and a drop of Homer's. For that you need the discerning—what Susan Sontag has called the "defending"—human eye. In "Against Interpretation," Sontag attempts to fine-tune the critic's attention, arguing for a paraphrasis that reveals *"how it is what it is"* (the "it" in this case being a work of art), rather than *"what it means."* In this paradigm there's an unstated moral faith that the critic, like the scientist, will use his genius in the service of good—that the reviewer in the Sunday book section doesn't have a bias for or against the writer under consideration—but right now I want to constrain my focus to the methods rather than the goals or "results" of criticism. For, putting aside questions of taste (on the part of the critic), vitality (on the part of the text), and, most importantly, motive (on both sides), exegesis stands as a recorded fantasizing, a written, orderly elaboration of the same process by which any reader enters a story and claims it for him- or herself. And even as we keep in mind Sontag's only slightly sarcastic admonition that "interpretation is the revenge of the intellect upon art," we must also remember that it is, in the most basic sense, *how people read*. Some readers see the history of Western civilization in *Ulysses*, others find it equally animate in an issue of the *X-Men*, and, though questions of taste and vitality come up in both instances—not to mention motive—you can't say either party is wrong.

That's the secret. The trick (what you might call keeping

the secret) is performing a bravura act of imaginative interpolation with a straight face. For example: "I've dropped my Brain," writes "Amherst's Madame de Sade"—aka Emily Dickinson, as Camille Paglia christened her in the unexpected critical bestseller *Sexual Personae*. Paglia went on to declare, "We hear a muffled thump, like the paperboy hitting the stoop with the evening edition." For Paglia and critics like her, a poem or story (or piece of art or other artifact) is less object than touchstone in the vast cultural subconscious, and she takes advantage of this nebulous state to push her readings beyond traditional limits of authorial intentionality or historical chronology. Exegesis at this level is less interpretation than parallel narrative, and sometimes it can be hard to tell if it expands a text's impact or diffuses it through too many tangential, anachronistic, esoteric associations. Or, to put it another way, whenever I see a critic taking such liberties I'm not sure if I'm in the presence of genius or insanity, but I sure do laugh a lot.

Which is, I'm pretty sure, the intention. Among other things, the humor of a Paglia or Wayne Koestenbaum or Dave Hickey makes conspicuous the subtle, easily ignored dramatic irony that informs all criticism. The idea that art—an enterprise whose primary function is to reveal the members of a culture to themselves—cannot be understood by that culture without Virgilian assistance would seem, on the face of it, absurd, and this particular brand of exegesis, while often way off the mark (if not simply off the wall), nonetheless acknowledges its supplemental relationship to the text in question; its humor is inviting, yet also invites its own dismissal. How sad, by comparison, is the critic who seems unaware of the inner workings of his own profession, who acts as if he is the only one who sees Waldo in the picture and can point him out to you.

Ladies and gentlemen, meet Sven Birkerts.

Birkerts first appeared on the critical scene with a 1979 examination of the work of Robert Musil. That first essay was particularly important to Birkerts, who on two separate occasions has cast its genesis as a lifelong endeavor: first, in the autobiographical second chapter of *The Gutenberg Elegies*, and then in the climactic chapter of his 2002 memoir, *My Sky Blue Trades*. Though he didn't "straightaway start grinding out essays by the basketful," he writes in the former book, that first essay did lead to "a change, a recognition"; in fact, he allows, "it reshaped my life to the very core." Almost shyly, he declares, "I liked my opening especially."

Indulge me for a moment:

> The career of Robert Musil excelled in disappointments and bitter ironies. Since his death—in exile and poverty—these disappointments and ironies have lived on; only now they are visited upon his readers, or more accurately, his prospective readers. For with the exception of a paperback reissue of *Young Törless* (1955), Musil's first published book, and the first volume (1953) of his gigantic, albeit unfinished, *The Man Without Qualities*, his works are difficult to find in this country. Volumes II and III of the latter work were published in the late 1950's only to be remaindered and, finally, pulped. For a time it was possible to obtain a volume of his stories, published variously as *Five Women* and *Tonka and Other Stories* (1966), but even a glowing preface by the likes of Frank Kermode was not sufficient to keep the book afloat in the treacherous waters of public demand. (The book was

reissued in 1986.) It seems that even now, decades after his death, the curse of obscurity still clings to Robert Musil.

If this were not indignity enough, there is still the fact that much of what Musil wrote waits to be translated. Two plays, *Die Schwärmer* and *Vinzenz oder Die Freundlin Bedeutender Männer*, and a prose collection, *Nachlass zu Lebzeiten*, lie undisturbed in their native language. The English title of this last might be: *The Posthumous Papers of a Living Author*, and is Musil's comment upon his own obscurity. He was himself bitter and incredulous, and he deeply resented the reputations achieved by writers like Thomas Mann and Hermann Broch. Musil could only assume that history would vindicate him and that he would be discovered by readers in the future. His assumption was not entirely in vain. Musil can claim more dedicated readers today than he could in his lifetime. But even so, the numbers are small. To the extent that this is owing to the neglect of the publishing industry, there is just no excuse. Such neglect is hardly excusable where lesser authors are concerned. But Musil is not a lesser author. He is one of the few great moderns, one of the handful who ventured to confront the issues that shape and define our time. To use a modern metaphor: he has a range and a striking capacity every bit as great as that of Mann, Joyce, or Beckett. The time is right for getting the whole of Musil translated and into print and for starting in on the work of clarifying his particular importance.

We must linger a moment longer on the subject of ironies and disappointments. . . .

"Every nation," T.S. Eliot wrote in "Tradition and the Individual Talent," "has not only its own creative, but its own critical turn of mind; and is even more oblivious of the shortcomings and limitations of its critical habits than of those of its creative genius." Forgive the excessive quotation, but I want you to have the unelided evidence to judge for yourself when I suggest that Sven Birkerts—winner of the National Book Critics Circle Citation for Excellence in Reviewing, a PEN Spielvogel/Diamondstein Special Citation, a Guggenheim Fellowship, and "one of six" recipients of a Lila Wallace–Reader's Digest Award—launched into his chosen profession of interpreter and tastemaker to the nation unable, like Alanis Morissette, to distinguish between irony and bad luck.[1]

2. I wrote my Peck stories . . .

If you were to pick up *My Sky Blue Trades* with little or no previous knowledge of Birkerts' work, as I did, you probably wouldn't realize how overdetermined the book is. Its tone is quiet, its presentation straightforward: Sven—called by what I think is his middle name, Peter, throughout—was born in the early fifties, to two parents, in the normal way, and lived long enough to write these words. No particularly garish or life-threatening or heroic experiences have marked his tenure on

---

[1] At some point in the intervening twenty-three years he's come to a clearer understanding, as witnessed by the eerily familiar introduction to his review of William Gaddis' *Agapé Agape* in the October 6, 2002, *New York Times Book Review:* "How deeply and regrettably ironic it is that the novelist who worked perhaps more ambitiously than any other to comprehend society's big picture—taking on finance, religion, the media and the ever-anxious relation of the artist to his culture—should himself be the least comprehended figure in our recent pantheon."

the planet, or at least until his twenty-seventh year, when the memoir ends. His parents were Latvian immigrants, and he spoke Latvian at home, giving him the conflicted dual identity of many bilingual American children. His preferred language was English though, and reading, he tells us, became a "compulsion" by the fourth grade, and soon enough he allowed himself to drift toward the idea of writing as well, trying his hand at poetry, then more studiously at fiction. Only when that didn't work out did he turn to criticism: enter Robert Musil.

In fact Birkerts has been preparing this story for nearly a decade. The second chapter of his 1996 book *The Gutenberg Elegies* is virtually a forty-page précis of the memoir, starting with Birkerts' childhood in Michigan with his Latvian parents and ending with the publication, at twenty-seven, of his first piece of criticism, on Robert Musil. If readers were wondering what an autobiographical essay had to do with "the fate of reading in an electronic age," *The Gutenberg Elegies'* ostensible subject, Birkerts answers the question in the first chapter of 1999's *Readings*. Here he refers to "a very particular sort of memoir" he's been working on, "the point of which is not to indulge in my recollections for their own sake, but rather to present them selectively in such a way that the reader will grasp my real point, which is that in the past fifty years or so something in the nature of time—or in our experience of it—has changed radically." In this transitional conception, *My Sky Blue Trades* is less memoir than "evidence," Birkerts' expert testimonial to the idea that "the human time experience may be undergoing a fundamental mutation." Birkerts isn't the first man to see in his own life a mirror of his times—*The Education of Henry Adams*, a text that reappears periodically in Birkerts' work, makes much the same claim for its subject—but he might be the first to declare it *before* writing his memoir, and then, on top of that, to abandon the idea in the actual book, where transhistorical analysis has less to do with the impact of the information revolution on "the human time experience" than with observations such as "living as we do in an era when various amphibians are under real threat of extinction, it's hard to imagine that there was once a staggering abundance of the creatures."

No, Birkerts' only subject here is himself, the inevitable progression from frog-killing child to book-killing critic. When he gets there, he weakly protests, as he did in *The Gutenberg Elegies*, that the significance he attached to his Musil essay was "misguided," even as he restates his belief that the essay was "some sort of rebirth." He does a little dance with modesty ("rebirth did not exactly follow—transformations are seldom so dramatic") then finally succumbs to his own conceit. "My whole life changed in a way that felt like part of a larger orchestration," he declares in the "coda" to his memoir, "as if somewhere, on high, a subtle but definite nod had been given." As if in proof, he offers the following anecdote:

> A few weeks after that baptism into print, while the ink was, figuratively speaking, still fresh on my fingers from so much endearing, then rapidly tiresome, handling of those pages, I was invited by my old bookstore friend Paul to a May Day party that some of his Marxist study-group comrades were giving. Not wanting to arrive dateless, I called Terri, but Terri was busy. Which turned out to be a providential thing for me. . . .

If you're thinking that Birkerts is about to meet his future wife at this party, you're correct. Yep: Birkerts finds his muse in the aesthetic sense, and "a few weeks" later finds her in the flesh as well. Causal connection? None. But "narratives unfailingly project lives as fates. Which is why so many of us resort to narratives: we want to feel carried in this way."

This, then, is the fatal narrative ostensibly carrying the reader through the 279 pages of dull sophistry that make *My Sky Blue Trades:* not "Growing Up Counter in a Contrary Time," as the consonance-crippled subtitle would have it, but rather "Portrait of the Artist as a Young Man." Or, more accurately, "Portrait of the Critic." Indeed, *My Sky Blue Trades* is in many ways a work of criticism itself, the next step in a twenty-year move away from simple book reviewing toward an ever-widening application of Birkerts' belief (following from Roland Barthes) "that popular culture yields wonders when subjected to academic modes of scrutiny." Consequently, *My Sky Blue Trades* reads less like memoir than biography, the Early Years of late-twentieth-century cultural critic Sven Birkerts, whose biographer is less concerned with narrating the events that occurred prior to the progenitive Musil essay than in "projecting" the narrative form, meaning, and inevitability to those events that would make the Musil essay their "unfailingly" logical outcome.

The origins of this particular idea occur even earlier than *The Gutenberg Elegies.* In a 1988 gloss of Pasternak's memoir *Safe Conduct,* Birkerts cites "the true nature" of Pasternak's "enterprise" as "an autobiography that would recover not what happened but what *mattered.*" And then again, in a 1994 essay entitled "Biography and the Dissolving Self," Birkerts writes,

"We attend to the particulars of the life as we read, but in some essential way we read *past* the defining circumstances and situations to make contact with the common—that is to say 'universal'—subject." "Biographical narration," Birkerts wrote two years before his first, hesitant attempt at writing his own,

> is premised on coherence and meaning. The biographer al-most occupationally views his subject as living under the as-pect of a singular destiny, with everything around him contributing to press his experience into its intended shape. Which of us feel [sic] some comparable sense of destination about our premillennial lives?

Here we find an echo of *My Sky Blue Trades'* notion that "narratives unfailingly project lives as fates," a quasi-Greek re-jection of the idea that will has anything to do with what hap-pens to us, not to mention the absurdly naive assumption that biographers capture the whole of a life in words, rather than just the parts that interest or are available to them. But, more importantly, we begin to see why Birkerts finds the idea so compelling. Our lives lack a "sense of destination." People today "are living provisionally, 'as if,' waiting again for the day to come when they will glimpse again what they may have be-held in younger days." Into this odd tautology ("waiting again . . . to . . . glimpse again") biography inserts a "continuum" of "common humanity" which "illuminate[s] facets of our own experience to ourselves." Biography, in other words, doesn't tell us about someone else's life, it tells us about our own. And what it tells us is how boring we are: "How will the lives of our present, which have lost the heft and distinctness of lives, get written? And, if written, who will want to read them?"

There's a lot that's problematic about this construction, not least Birkerts' condescending generalization that people today "have lost the heft and distinctness of lives," or the fact that his notion of readerly projection is, on the most basic level, a misapplication of the way people read fiction to the way they read nonfiction, but perhaps worst of all, in the case of the biography under consideration, is the fact that it's a pretty accurate description of the way Birkerts has read (and written) his own life in *My Sky Blue Trades*. The existence that preceded the Robert Musil essay—i.e., "the defining circumstances and situations" of its author's life, or "what happened"—is referred to, even described over the course of 270 pages, but any empathic connection to those events is continually undercut by a critical lens that "reads past" the particulars in search of the "universal" or "what mattered": "this is a very common American story"; "we glimpse so many things growing up, but it can take decades before we know how to read them"; "we all know the comic camera renditions of the drinker's progress"; "The occasion? I forget, nor does it matter"; "I will not even try to describe the first day." "The drama is not manifest," Birkerts tells us on page 19: "it is to be inferred." Which is, the reader understands by memoir's end, a slightly longer way of saying that the drama is not manifest.

Birkerts, in other words, isn't re-viewing his life in *My Sky Blue Trades*, he's reviewing it in much the same way he reviews fiction, telling his readers what they can learn from the text of his life. This sort of pedagogy would be dull from just about anyone, but coming from someone who seems to have done a little bit less than the average man of his day—a vaguely liberal drug-taking coming of age in the sixties and seventies punctuated by a not-exactly-Casanovaesque spate of failed relationships and artistic endeavors—it was particularly boring, and at some point during the course of Birkerts' dithering twenties I found myself reading past all the hazily rendered "defining circumstances" and trying to imagine what "common humanity" linked the two of us. What facet of my own experience might I find illuminated in so much plodding, slightly embarrassing exposure of one man's early failures? What seemed to me most interesting about Birkerts—his Latvian heritage and his immigrant parents, especially his father, an architect who worked with "Eero" (as in " 'Eero' this and 'Eero' that") and "Bob" Venturi and "Charlie" Eames—is casually, if not cruelly, dismissed. The young Peter was terrified of his father, which suggests that the man might have done something to make his son so afraid of him, but the adult Sven allows the offense to exist by insinuation, offering only the symbolically pat accusation that his father was "not a reader at all" and therefore incapable of understanding his son, to wit:

> He is looking at me as if he can take in only my most basic outline, as if the rest of his focus is still en route.
> 'Pete—'

But a more active reading experience acquired sudden, dramatic possibility when I encountered the following passage late in *My Sky Blue Trades:* "It was the Hemingway of the Nick Adams stories who got me thinking that I could write fiction. . . . I had my own Nick Adams stand-in, Peck, and over a period of about two years I gave him a world, a life, more or less coextensive with my own." Perhaps it was merely the presence of my own name in the text, but something about these words pricked at me. By that point, I should add, I had already put down the memoir once to read *An Artificial Wilderness*, Birkerts' first book of essays, and this Peck continued to taunt me as I made my way through the rest of Birkerts' oeuvre. There he was again in *The Gutenberg Elegies:* "Peck was a young man living on the fringes, waiting for real life to send him something worthy. . . . Nothing ever happened to the fellow—nothing of note. He was trapped by his creator, who was himself trapped in the long loop of college, impatient for his life to really begin." He is waiting for something "fictionworthy." Those words came immediately to mind when I encountered Birkerts' thesis that people today are waiting to "glimpse again what they may have beheld in younger days." And what was it they beheld? "A map, a track, a defining sense of how they fit into the world." But now we realize that this map was not in fact ever present in the young Birkerts' life, and as such the supposed "glimpse" of it that readers get in his biography is an invented one. The Peck stories taught the aspiring artist Peter that his life was not "fictionworthy," but, ironically enough, it was "Biography and the Dissolving Self" that taught the established critic Sven that it didn't matter: he could invent a new life for himself under the guise of "universality," one in which his true "destination," his divinely guided "fate," was not to be a novelist but a critic. Birkerts doesn't attempt to disguise the fact that these "destinies" and "narratives" aren't real, are nothing more than the "need" or "want" of someone whose "premillennial life," by his own admission, lacked the direction of a Caesar, or even a

C.S. Lewis. But it was only after I had charted its inception through Birkerts' earlier work that I was able to see that *My Sky Blue Trades* is a fakebook, by which I don't mean that it is the sketched chords of a symphony that doesn't sound on its pages, but rather that the story it *does* tell is deceitful and self-serving—as are, in the end, the hundreds of essays that had preceded and produced it.

"How could I ever tell my father—I never have—that the erratic flaring of his moods, his incessant swerves in and out of temper, created the very weather of home and are now part of the core deposit of my childhood?" If you sift through the relentlessly mixed metaphors (flaring, swerves, weather, deposits—I mean *really*) what you find here is more of Birkerts' ignorance of how irony (in this case of the dramatic variety) works. But here the ignorance feels feigned; his "I never have" is one protest too many, and I'm sure he knows, as do his readers, that this passage is exactly "how" Pete has finally managed to "tell" his father how much he hurt him, and to humiliate the pater publicly in the process. And it is this same revenge disguised as goodwill that informs essay after essay, interpretation after interpretation, as Birkerts takes out his failure as a novelist on the very thing he professes to love. "The revenge of the intellect upon art" indeed: if he can't write it, he'll kill it. But *My Sky Blue Trades* did succeed on one level. Birkerts had finally, if unwittingly, given his Peck something to say. He would mount literature's counterattack against false exegesis.

And here, before I get into making my case against the Birkertian method, I suppose I should detail my full history with Birkerts' writing for the reader who suspects some prior relationship. I first encountered Birkerts when I read his review of David Foster Wallace's *Infinite Jest* and chose to quote (ironically, as it happens) a line of his praise which I thought adequately characterized one of that novel's flaws. Whether Birkerts saw the quotation is unknown to me, but he was recently forthright enough to remark that "reviews like [mine] subtly degrade the profession." I'd like to take this opportunity to apologize if there was any misunderstanding. I wasn't trying to be subtle.

CAN YOU HEAR ME NOW?

Good.

3. If you find it, it's probably there . . .

Let me state the obvious and get it out of the way: Sven Birkerts really loves books. His life is dedicated to reading books and to getting more people to read books (if I am repetitive here, it's because Birkerts loathes the idea of reading on a screen; if you're looking at this review online, Birkerts would argue, you're not *really* reading it). His program is as well-intentioned as they come.

And now let us move beyond that. Birkerts doesn't love individual books so much as he loves the edifice of literature and his own conception of himself as a small but integral part of that edifice—the keyhole, say, maybe even the doorknob. His writing is full of geriatric enthusiasm, an enthusiasm that, spread out over an oeuvre, is touching, almost charming. Reading Birkerts, especially when he writes about contemporary novelists or the Internet, I feel like I'm watching an old man tapping his foot to a phat beat, maybe even letting himself lip sync the words *muthafuckin bitches, muthafuckin hos* (hell, even I feel old when I write shit like that). And when he's writing about his beloved early-twentieth-century moderns, it's as if the channel has switched to a polka station and the old man gets up and parties.

Am I being dismissive? Yes, of course. But it's hard not to be. Birkerts cut his teeth in the Reagan era with reviews of Musil, Osip Mandelstam, Michel Tournier, Robert Walser, Blaise Cendrars, Joseph Roth, Max Frisch, Gregor von Rezzori, Heinrich Böll, Jorge Luis Borges, Malcolm Lowry—writers, in other words, whose best work had come two, three, four decades earlier. Though many of the essays take the revivalist stance of the Musil piece, it's hard not to conclude, in the wake of so many reexaminations, that Birkerts seemed not to have realized when he wrote these pieces that times and tastes had changed. That, in fact, the modern canon was no longer adequate to dissecting "the issues that shape and define our time," which is why we'd had postmodernism, and whatever it is that's taking shape in the wake of postmodernism. The writers Birkerts focused on—with the exception of Borges—weren't the animating forces that Woolf or Joyce or Melville or the Brontës were, or Cervantes, or Dante, or Ovid, or Homer; they were by and large good writers whose work had receded into historical context.

Those reviews were gathered in 1987's *An Artificial Wilderness: Essays on Twentieth Century Literature.* Four more books have followed: *The Electric Life: Essays on Modern Poetry; American Energies: Essays on Fiction; The Gutenberg Elegies: The Fate of Reading in an Electronic Age;* and *Readings,* which includes pieces culled from the former books as well as new material which revisits its various subjects. He has also edited an anthology, *Tolstoy's Dictaphone: Technology and the Muse.*

Taken as a career, the books' trajectory has a visible—one wants to say telling—arc. In his first two collections, Birkerts set himself up as a kind of literary historian, reviewing writers whose place in the canon, even if marginal or commercially unsuccessful, was nevertheless not in question; many are Nobel laureates, others "perennial Nobel candidate[s]." Throughout those early essays, Birkerts is wont to compare contemporary fiction pejoratively with the classics he's reviewing, even as contemporary writing gradually, if haphazardly, became an increasingly large part of his focus. In *American Energies,* his third book, it's easy to see Birkerts scrambling for assignments, taking whatever comes his way until, by the early nineties, he had reversed his fogeyism and established himself as a cheerleader for the most celebrated novelists of the day. For example, Birkerts dismissed William Gaddis and Don DeLillo as part of the postmodern plague that has "infected" all the arts in his 1986 essay "An Open Invitation to Extraterrestrials," but completely reversed his position by the time of his 1998 review of *Underworld,* in which he says that DeLillo has given us nothing less than "a new way to think" (and Gaddis, of course, has been revived as a figure whose under-appreciation, presumably by critics like the young Birkerts, is "deeply and regrettably ironic"). This transformation seems to have springboarded off Tom Wolfe's 1989 manifesto "Stalking the Billion-Footed Beast," an essay (and, for that matter, a writer) Birkerts can't resist citing even as he can't resist mocking him ("Still, his misconceptions, so starkly posed, help to clarify the terms of the discussion"); the primary source of his fascination seems to be that Wolfe's program, however flawed, was significantly more popular than Birkerts' own ("True, Wolfe was as much proselytizing his own vision as passing judgment on others, but the splash was considerable").

By 2001, Birkerts' anti-postmodern sentiments had been jettisoned as the byproduct of a "great populist prejudice" he's now, thankfully, outgrown. He had discovered in contemporary fiction—that is, "William Gass, Don DeLillo, Cormac McCarthy, Cynthia Ozick, Harold Brodkey, Annie Proulx, Toni Morrison, Paul West, and Maureen Howard, as well as short-story acrobats Barry Hannah, Denis Johnson, and Thom Jones," and also including everything from "David Foster Wallace (*Infinite Jest*) to Richard Powers (*Galatea 2.2, Plowing the Dark*) to Donald Antrim (*The Verificationist*) to Helen DeWitt (*The Last Samurai*) to Rick Moody (*Purple America*) to Colson Whitehead (*John Henry Days*) to Jonathan Franzen (*The Corrections*), and on and on," by which he seems to mean "DeLillo, Proulx, Ozick, Howard, Michael Chabon, Michael Cunningham, Brad Leithauser, Steven Millhauser, Alice Munro, and Michael Ondaatje," and also "Chang-rae Lee in *A Gesture Life*, or Jhumpa Lahiri in *The Interpreter of Maladies*," and, lest we forget, "Updike, Roth, and Bellow," and of course "Thomas Pynchon" and "William Gaddis"—"the first reflection" of a "larger transformation in consciousness," namely, "a common expansive will: to embrace, to mime, to unfold [by which I think he means "enfold"] in the cadence of a sentence the complexities of life as lived."

In his effort to word his thesis broadly enough to include as many popular authors as possible (and to avoid using the term "postmodern"), Birkerts seemed to be casting himself in a kind of Harold Bloom role as definer and guardian of the Western canon. And the one writer he's most interested in excluding from that canon? None other than the man who inspired him to his first, failed efforts at writing fiction: Ernest Hemingway. His earlier adoration is now recast as a "prejudice," one he "imbibed" at his schools and which, he hastens to add, spreading the blame, he "was far from alone in believing" (in fact, Birkerts couldn't resist a final stab at fiction in his review of Hemingway's posthumous *True at First Light*, which he casts in the form of an interview with Papa's ghost, "an old guy in a Hawaiian shirt and blind-man glasses" who shows up for the interview drunk). But since "minimalism," as Birkerts categorizes the style of Hemingway's "followers," hardly constitutes a substantial nemesis, Birkerts instead established himself as the de facto enemy of the electronic age, devoting the entirety of his fourth book, *The Gutenberg Elegies*, to a series of screeds detailing how electronic media "threaten" the "frail set of balances" of what Birkerts calls the "ecology of reading." In its paper good–screen bad dichotomy, *The Gutenberg Elegies* courts exactly the same kind of popular controversy that Wolfe caught in his "Stalking the Billion-Footed Beast," a controversy that, ironically, seemed only to interest the most die-hard advocates of the new media technologies.

In all of this I imagine that Birkerts is, in his way, an editor's dream. Need somebody to slog through a second-rate translation of Mandelstam's journals or *The Radetzky March* and produce two thousand words to fill that big slot in the middle of the book—for not very much money to boot? Birkerts is your man. Want someone who will mulch his way through all of Gaddis (and Franzen snatched up by the *New Yorker*, darn it)? Hey, let's call Sven. For, if Birkerts' theses don't remain consistent, his awe of his own words, of the power he ascribes to them and the profundities which he thinks they contain ("something in the nature of time—or in our experience of it— has changed radically") is unshakable. He can take the tiniest premise and stretch it out like a child smearing that last tea-spoon of peanut butter over a piece of bread, unaware it's spread so thin that it no longer has any taste. But at the end of the day, despite the hyperbole that characterizes most of his es-says ("one of the few great moderns"; "the issues that shape and define our time"; "a striking capacity every bit as great as that of Mann, Joyce, or Beckett"), there exists between Birkerts' criticism and the writing it describes a measured rally of fic-tional trope and critical affirmation that's about as interesting to watch as a game of Pong in which neither player moves his paddle and the ball shuttles back and forth between them in a horizontal line: *bip . . . bip . . . bip . . . bip*. These are great writ-ers, Birkerts says time and again, that only I, the great critic, can explain to you.

Not that the man is without his skills. One of the things Birkerts does do well is render straightforward information in prose, turning lists into sentences. Look again at the catalog of Musil's work, the way the titles are given variously in English, German, or both, the occasional descriptive tag thrown in as punctuation ("gigantic, albeit unfinished"; "only to be remain-dered and, finally, pulped"). That's lively stuff, or as lively as these sorts of things can get. They reflect the sensibility of a man who loves facts, appreciates them even, no matter how trivial or misplaced they might be (what matters is that Musil's books were unread, not that they were "remaindered and, fi-nally, pulped," but the aside adds color and weight to the event,

giving readers a physical object whose loss is easier to visualize
than a book they likely haven't read).

Birkerts also does a good plot summary:

> The Trotta family was awarded its honorary "von" after the
> Battle of Solferino, in the middle years of the nineteenth cen-
> tury. Young Lieutenant Trotta, acting on courageous im-
> pulse, saved the emperor Francis Joseph from a bullet. The
> Trotta name was promptly inscribed on the emperor's list;
> so long as the Austro-Hungarian Monarchy endured, pro-
> tection and patronage would never be denied.
>
> The lieutenant, uncomfortable with new rank and title,
> retires into provincial obscurity, ceding the stage to his son.
> Franz von Trotta, all rectitude and righteousness, is the
> first to break with the family's military tradition. . . .

Here are dozens of pages of fiction compressed into a few
lines. Even without knowing what book they describe (Joseph
Roth's *Radetzky March*) the events are clear and don't require
context, and there's even a bit of (dare I say it?) dramatic irony
in that "so long as the Austro-Hungarian Monarchy endured."
As it happens, I think that these are two of the most important
weapons in any critic's arsenal, and, if I can work Birkerts'
"modern metaphor" a little further, if he had stuck to them he
wouldn't have lost half as many battles as he has.

But Birkerts wants to do more than merely bring books to
readers. He wants to tell readers how they should be reading
them. He doesn't want to represent the canon, he wants to *explain* it. But explanations, alas, are not Birkerts' strong suit:

> The sources of Roth's particular power are hard to pin
> down. Neither plot nor character will account for it. True,

the district commissioner emerges as a compelling figure—
his fidelity takes on a tragic dimension as the novel progresses; but Carl Joseph is the very reverse. He is a husk, a
frightened, self-occupied failure. His decline is inevitable,
and we can even take a certain pleasure in watching it.
But this is not when the novel achieves its greatness. No, the
pity and terror are felt when we realize that Carl Joseph is
a transparency, that we are looking right through him at
the impersonal rush of history. His emptiness turns out
to be a precise emblem of the moral vacuum of the
times.

First, Birkerts tells us that Roth's power is "hard to pin
down," so that when he tries to pin it down readers understand
that he is attempting a difficult task on our behalf. He rejects
plot and character, and then investigates character and plot
("He is a husk . . . His decline is inevitable") just to make
sure. But "this is not when the novel achieves it greatness." We
are confused. What could it be, then? And then suddenly: symbolism! The character isn't *real*, but is rather "a precise emblem" (not just any emblem, mind you, but a *precise* emblem)
of "the impersonal rush of history" (again, not just any history,
but the impersonal rushing kind). What we are witness-
ing here is either a critic pretending to dramatize his discovery
of the use of a pretty standard literary device, or, even worse,
actually discovering symbolism for the first time. There's
nothing "hard to pin down" about symbolism—which doesn't
at all lessen its impact on readers—but Birkerts seems not to
realize that the difficulty lies not in the reader's spotting it in
the text but in the writer's creation of a concrete and compelling stand-in for something large and amorphous—which

is, in fact, the real source of Roth's particular power (not just *any* power . . .).

Note also how Birkerts' already rather stiff prose tends to break down as he gives in to these exegetical flights of fancy. The sentences grow simultaneously more turgid and cliché-ridden, all of which serves to obscure the fact that he is for all intents and purposes talking out of his ass. My particular favorite (in reference to Keats' "Ode to Autumn"):

> Observe, first, what the mouth must do to vocalize the line: "Season of mists and mel-low fruit-ful-ness." The lips widen and stretch to make the initial *ee* sound in "Season," contract the same position to pronounce "mists," and contract it yet again, just slightly to form the syllable "mel-." If we think of these contractions as representing diminishing circumferences—as, say, cross sections of a funnel—then with the small *o* of "-low" and the *oo* of "fruit-" (which cannot be made without a pouting protrusion of the lips and an even smaller aperture) we have come to the narrowed apex. This would not necessarily be significant in itself, but when we consider the unstated physical process—the moisture being siphoned out of the soil and into the fruit through the myriad fine roots, the push against gravity—then these lip movements become instrumental.
>
> But this is not all. There is also a simultaneous *lingual* event. For in order to enunciate cleanly the words "mel-low fruit-ful-ness" the tip of the tongue must sketch out the shape of a fruit. . . .

The only way I can think of responding to this passage is with Birkerts' own words: "You're hired," as he and his male friends liked to say in junior high "every time someone blew out a match." The word Birkerts can't bring himself to type here is "blowjob," and it puts a whole new spin on the idea of the tongue sketching a fruit.

But it doesn't stop there. When you sift through the inanity of Birkerts' exegeses, what you find is a slew of grammatical, citational, and cultural errors, starting with his misplaced "irony" in the first paragraph of his first review and continuing through *My Sky Blue Trades*, where there is, among other things, the almost poignantly beautiful ignorance of "nowadays"—by which Birkerts seems to mean *Happy Days*— "the word for Howard would be 'nerd.'" Writing on Tom Wolfe's *A Man in Full*, he remarked, "In art, as in horseshoes, close doesn't count," when the expression is in fact "almost *only* counts in horseshoes and hand grenades" (in horseshoes, a ringer is worth three points, a horseshoe that touches the pole is worth two, and any horseshoe that lands within six inches of the pole is worth one). And then there are those "endangered amphibians" mentioned earlier. For Birkerts' edification, of the four endangered species of frog in the United States (the California red-legged, the Chiricahua leopard, the Mississippi gopher, and the mountain yellow-legged), three live in the Southwest and one in the Mississippi delta; none are anywhere near Michigan.

The problem lies less with the mistakes—nobody except perhaps Birkerts himself actually expects him to know as much as Harold Bloom—than with the obviousness with which Birkerts trots out his supposed displays of erudition in order to invest himself with authority. He is, for example, fond of allusions—so fond that he often repeats himself. On at least two separate occasions he references Erasmus' anecdote of finding a printed page of prose on the road to, I think, Wittenberg. Twice also he tells us how surprised St. Augustine was to see someone reading without moving his lips, and twice that the word "history" is a cognate with "story"; on at least three occasions he alludes to Pascal's "The heart has its reasons which reason knows nothing of."

The wording of these allusions is itself clumsy, as if they've been shoehorned into his reviews like the stepsisters' feet into Cinderella's slipper:

"It has, like Nietzsche's God, been finished off."

"The play's the thing—but will it be?"

"Reading in the early age of print was, for a host of reasons, different from reading in the age of mechanical reproduction."

"I see Old Nick winking and I find myself wondering if we might not indeed be ready to push onto [sic] something new, to put behind us once and for all this melancholy business of isolated selves trudging through a vale of tears."

Some of these allusions are questionable. For example, was Birkerts consciously invoking James Montgomery's vale of tears, or just using it because it sounded familiar, maybe even Biblical? And then there is the "What is to be done?" that comes in the course of one of many essays about how to resist the information revolution. Though the stilted, slightly old-fashioned phrasing seems to suggest that he intended the Lenin allusion (which is itself an allusion to Nikolai Chernyshevsky's nineteenth-century novel of the same name), Birkerts' prose is in general stilted and slightly old-fashioned, and it wouldn't surprise me to learn that he had neither Lenin nor Chernyshevsky in mind when he wrote these words. Another

of Birkerts' allusions that interests me might also be uninten-
tional: "The novel was to be a kind of petri dish," he wrote in an
essay called "Second Thoughts," "in which the novelist would
explore the ever-changing terms of 'how it is.' " Is this a deliberate reference to the penultimate sentence of "Against Interpretation"? I can only guess that it is—Birkerts makes frequent
reference to Sontag, especially in his early essays—and if that's
the case then it's illuminating, given that Birkerts' entire program upholds the exegetical tropes of ignoring what's on the
page in favor of what the critic supposedly unmasks behind it, a
proposition that stands directly at odds with Sontag's thesis.

And sometimes Birkerts gets even the allusion wrong. "An-
tonio Gramsci's often-cited sentence comes inevitably to
mind," he writes in *The Gutenberg Elegies* (note how "often-
cited" and "inevitably" insinuate Birkerts' membership in an
elite network of Gramsci readers and aphorists, one that com-
pels you to ask if *you* belong): " 'The crisis consists precisely in
the fact that the old is dying and the new cannot be born; in this
interregnum a great variety of morbid symptoms appears.' " I
can only speculate here, but I'm willing to bet that lines from
Gramsci are rarely remembered (especially verbatim) by anyone outside of Marxist reading groups (to which Birkerts
might or might not have belonged, as evidenced by how he met
his wife); but at any rate the writer who is in fact "often-cited"
here is not Gramsci but Matthew Arnold, who wrote in 1855,
thirty-six years before Gramsci was born: "Wandering between two worlds, one dead,/ The other powerless to be born,/
With nowhere yet to rest my head." It was Gramsci who was
making the allusion, not Birkerts, and Gramsci who trusted
enough in his reader's abilities that he didn't have to name-

drop Matthew Arnold's "often-cited" "Stanzas From the Grande Chartreuse." But, for Birkerts' sake if not yours, I will mention that all of my information, from the definition of irony to the list of endangered species of North American frogs, is culled from three sources: the Columbia *Encyclopedia, Bartlett's Familiar Quotations,* and Google.com.

Birkerts trots out all his allusions and factlets and trivia, regardless of accuracy, relevance, or extraneousness, with the tinkling insistence of a five-year-old learning to play "Chopsticks." With each rendition he bangs louder and louder, as if to conceal the fact that he doesn't know how to play anything else. In his catch-as-catch-can imitation of New Critical methods, he ignores or is ignorant of the full history of literature on the part of both author and audience, and also, indeed, of the "common" character of the artist—particularly the American artist he once aspired to be and now aspires to understand. D.H. Lawrence, writing on Herman Melville seventy-five years ago, got that character out in a pair of sentences. "It is the same old thing as in all Americans. They keep their old-fashioned ideal frock-coat on, and an old-fashioned silk hat, while they do the most impossible things." Birkerts has the stodginess, if not simply the snobbiness of the frock-coat tone down pat. But he is unable to make it sparkle as critics such as Daniel Mendelsohn and Darryl Pinckney and James Wood do, as Sontag and Bloom and Elizabeth Hardwick have done, as Edmund Wilson did, or Lawrence, or T.S. Eliot. "There are many people who appreciate the expression of sincere emotion in verse," Eliot wrote in his most famous essay on literature, "and there is a smaller number of people who can appreciate technical excellence." Eliot was a stick in the mud, and that sentence is about as grammatically pedantic as they come; but he was also one of the most galvanic forces in the history of English literature, and his insistence upon the agreement of subject and verb regardless of the discordance wrought by a prepositional object is his top-hat-and-tails way of saying fuck you to readers, writers, and critics who can't see beyond such pedantry. Which of us *feels*, I would ask Mr. Birkerts, some comparable sense of destination when we encounter the finite but real energy released when syntax unites with content to yield more than mere meaning?

Or, to put it another way (ready, Sven? I've been saving this one up since the end of the last section), with friends like this, literature needs an enema.

Ooh, that was probably a bit much, huh?

4. *They taught what, as a rule, needed no teaching . . .*

It is a large oeuvre. Six books, hundreds of essays. The temptation is to refute each one individually, to point out how Birkerts gets it wrong or stamps his flag of "discovery" right through a native foot. I've jotted down dozens of *bonnes ripostes* that are going to waste.

But to engage with the arguments is, at the end of the day, to give them more credence than they deserve. As far as I can tell (and I'm willing to bet that, with the exception of the author himself, I've read more of Birkerts' work than anyone else on the planet), Birkerts' entire program is on evidence in this rhetorical exchange in his review of Wolfe's *A Man in Full*:

There has been a misunderstanding. Somewhere, I sense, the mass of American readers has gotten the idea not only that Wolfe is fashionable but also that his work is legitimate literature. Updike notwithstanding, people have begun to believe that they can enjoy themselves and be doing some serious cultural lifting at the same time. After all, Updike did write about [*A Man in Full*], as did Harold Bloom in the pages of the *New York Observer*, so it must have something to do with art, right?

Sorry, no. The bad news is that it doesn't happen that way. Serious art is only enjoyable up to a point, and then it becomes work: perceiving, judging, and knowing. Yes, these things can give pleasure, but of a different sort; they are pleasures that push us against the grain of our ease. If it's too much fun, it can't be art. Nor will it quite do to say that a novel like Wolfe's comes close. In art, as in horseshoes, close doesn't count.

I almost feel sorry for the poor man as I read him describing literature as though it were a bran muffin pushing "against the grain of our ease" (even as I want to point out that you don't push against the grain, you rub against it), but the truth is I feel more sympathy for "the mass of American readers" who have "imbibed" exactly the same message, and as a result feel excluded from literature as well as other forms of "serious" art. These readers, who might or might not be part of what Birkerts once referred to as "the more desirable demographic" (aka, "the upper middle class"), are, in his estimation, incapable of participating in "reading in its purest form," which he characterizes as an impassioned, intellectual engagement with "the literary novel." While I'm willing to give him that some novels

are better than others, I don't think that the quality of a novel
has anything to do with the quality of the reading experience;
if anything, the average reader of genre fiction is significantly
more committed to his or her books than is the benumbed consumer of couture literature. To paraphrase Mark Van Doren,
"Harry Potter is a world; Virginia Woolf a style."

I would argue, in fact, that contemporary readers—not to
mention contemporary writers—responding to the tutelage of
freewheeling critics such as Birkerts (who has written "if you
find it, it's probably there," with, as far as I can tell, no irony at
all), have lost the crucial distinction between projection and
identification. This marks a fundamental shift in the way fiction is read and written, and strikes me as having a far more
devastating impact on the future of the novel than television or
the Internet. Birkerts had it half right in "Biography and the
Dissolving Self": reading (fiction at any rate) is a process of
discovering something in a story and measuring your own life
against that yardstick. But the majority of today's novelists—
from recidivist realists to recherché postmodernists—have
long since ceased providing readers with anything to measure
themselves against. Like Birkerts, they write as though the in-
vocation of universal tropes or universal themes is all it takes to
tell a universal story, and as a result, instead of identifying with
what he or she encounters on the page, today's reader is forced
to project the content into fiction. The novel has become a
screen not for the novelist's subconscious, but readers', and
they are spurred on in this process by blinkered critics such as
Birkerts. His work, lacking even the take-it-or-leave-it premise
of the significantly wackier readings of avant-garde theorists
like Paglia or Koestenbaum, calls to mind the Talmudic and

Biblical connotations of exegesis, in which rabbinical scholars and priests attempted to channel their congregants' faith by means of interpretation of the Scriptures, much of which interpretation claimed to be as divinely guided as the words it supposedly explained. This is exegesis of the give-a-man-a-fish kind. Its purveyors do not want to teach anything, lest they find themselves out of a job.

Or, to invoke Sontag's paradigm, it shows *"what it means"* to the exclusion of *"how it is what it is."* There's an opposition in Sontag's paradigm that I don't think is really necessary, but at least it's there for a reason. In her heartfelt appeal for the discrete individuality of Blanche DuBois, Sontag was reacting to critics who, like Birkerts, project their notion of *"what it means"* on a work of art, even if it stood at odds with *"how it is what it is."* But much of Sontag's work—her fiction as well as her criticism—stands as a testament to the "erotics" of meaning, in which *"how it is what it is"* and *"what it means"* are conflated—combined and commuted—into something we might simply call *what it is*.

As it happens, I've been looking for a contemporary critic's work to discuss for some time (for far longer, if you're wondering, than I've known about Birkerts' memoir). I've been lambasting today's fiction for a while now, but, as over-rated and misguided as most of our celebrated novelists are, it seems to me that the fault isn't entirely theirs, but must also be vested to some degree in those who praise them for their efforts. In this regard, a better target would have been Heidi Julavits, who is an even worse critic than she is a novelist, but her Orwellian screed had yet to appear in *The Believer* when I initially set out to write this piece. And, at any rate, it was Sven Birkerts' name that rose to the top of the list as the critic who most represents the offensive banalities of the worst mainstream reviewing combined with the defensive pieties of the "best" haute criticism. He is by no means the only culprit, but he does seem to be the most prolific and the most sanctimonious, the lowest common denominator of the American critical establishment. To the degree that Birkerts has borne the brunt of my anger at an entire industry, I apologize, but I'm sure he can content himself with imagining the kind of reviews *my* next book is going to get. But that's neither here nor there, as is, as far as I'm concerned, yet another self-indulgent memoir dropped onto the dung heap that particular genre has become. The point is that when Birkerts writes that "ephemeral work ultimately holds the idea of art in contempt," it seems to me that a critic whose own hands are stained with so much carelessly spilled ink ought to be more careful about the mud he flings.

Literature does have its enemies, and chief among them are pseudointellectual artists and critics who think their love of books translates into some kind of knowledge. Ultimately, Birkerts is nothing more than a snob without the credentials to back it up. A quarter-century ago, as his memoir confirms, he turned to criticism because he couldn't write fiction; and all those years of reviews have demonstrated is that at least one of the reasons why he failed as a novelist is because *he just doesn't understand the form.* That he has hitched his yoke to a group of equally bombastic and befuddled writers is fitting and also tragic. Together they are carting the "experimental" novel on its tumbrel to the guillotine. If that's all they kill, more power to them. But chances are they will alienate more and more readers from all fiction—and I don't mean Birkerts' mythological proletariat who are just waiting for someone to show them why *The Waves* is more rewarding than *The Chamber of Secrets*, but the members of the educated bourgeoisie, who are sick and tired of feeling like they've somehow failed the modern novel.

For far longer than books have had covers—for far longer than there have been books—their essence has not been contained in their pages. I am talking, unironically, about something ineffable, alchemical, mystical: the potent cocktail of writer and reader and language, of intention and interpretation, conscious and unconscious, text, subtext, and context, narrative, character, metaphor. Not one of these constructs is any more stable than the atoms that make up a glass tumbler, and yet, somehow, they manage to contain a story, a meaning that transcends the reading experience, that permeates, indeed guides, all of culture. In crass capitalist terms, books are entertainment's cheapest feeder industry; in the grandest metaphysical sense they are the reference library of our souls, and they share that power with all art forms: music, theater, painting, sculpture, and those which combine them: dance, film, installation and performance art, and the ever-evolving electronic and "interactive" (as if all art isn't already) media. One of Birkerts' biggest problems is that he never addresses other art forms, other modes of "inwardness," of discovering the self and the world. Like a true child of the Enlightenment, he believes in a rational, mappable psyche and omits from his purview all evidence of the irrational, or what is inexplicable by rational, linguistic terms. In this he not only sells short all writing, but art itself. He ignores the basic revelation of his own meditations on reading—that literature isn't just about words—and instead

tries, with his pseudocritical rationality, to "explain" everything.

"The whole art—fiction, poetry, and drama—is fundamentally pledged to coherence," writes the same critic who
later asked of himself, "Why am I such a bad Latvian?" It's notable that a critic who began his career with a plea for the translation of work by Robert Musil and other great writers has to
the best of my knowledge never translated or, for that matter,
written about the work of a single Latvian writer. Birkerts' essays are full of rhetorical questions, but for some reason this
one stayed with me, probably because he never tries to answer
it, at least not "coherently." But the silence surrounding that
unanswered question resonates throughout his memoir, as in
this exchange with Joseph Brodsky, whom Birkerts befriended
after the poet came into a bookstore where the young Peter
worked:

> But then, later, I did ask Brodsky if he knew any Latvian
> poets.
>   "There are no Latvian poets."
>   "Rainis—"
>   "*Rainis . . .*" He laughed cruelly and I cringed. "Ya, Rai-
> nis." That was all.
>   At that moment I surprised in myself a spark of ancient
> chauvinism. I felt the ancestral culture being mocked, and
> I—who had so resolutely refused all things Latvian—felt
> hurt. I wanted to rush forth in defense. I should have,
> though I can't imagine what I might have said. But instead I
> let it go. So eager was I to claim the poet as a friend that I let
> his cynical posturing silence me. I carefully steered the con-
> versation back to safer ground.

And there it has stayed ever since. Birkerts' "ancestral culture," as indeed "all things Latvian," has disappeared from his
work in every respect save one:

His name.

"I was, at least on the first day of school every year, before I
instructed my teacher to call me 'Pete,' Sven." The child Pete
felt being Latvian—being Sven—"barred me from being an
American," just as the young man Pete felt that an admiration
for Janis Rainis barred him from the world of literature Brodsky represented, just as, I assume, the fully grown Sven es-
chews translating Latvian literature: because it's not the kind
of thing that will gain him entry into the world of American
letters he wants so desperately to be a citizen of. Birkerts tells
us that his rebirth began with the publication of his first essay,
"slow, steady, rejuvenating change, and all of it was somehow
connected to the extraordinary lift I felt when I at last rounded
the corner of Out-of-Town News and saw the small pile of
freshly minted copies of the *New Boston Review*, the headline
ROBERT MUSIL'S ATLANTIS prominent above the fold." It
was only after I'd read and reread that paragraph a dozen times
that I realized the writer never tells us what name—beyond
Musil's—was attached to it. By which I mean that at memoir's
end we've learned how Birkerts became a critic—he was, indeed, born to be one—but we never find out how he became
Sven.

2

To P. or Not to P.

Infinite Jest by David Foster Wallace

I'm going to go out on a limb and claim that the U.S. literary world can be divided into two camps: those who think Thomas Pynchon is a very clever guy, and those who also think he's a great writer. As it happens, I'm of the former camp. While I admit that Pynchon's writing is packed with all sorts of ideas, ultimately the novels strike me as more crudités than smorgasbord: the appetizers keep coming (and coming, and coming), but the main course never arrives. Pynchon's hallmarks are his tentacular—I might almost say amorphous—prose, which can and does snare just about any philosophical concept or pop cultural phenomenon in its grasp; and his sense of satire, which can be awfully funny if your taste runs to broad humor, which mine does. Neither of these traits is necessarily damning, but it's Pynchon's particular conflation of them that's always limited his appeal for me. Given a choice between pathos and bathos, Pynchon errs on the side of farcical melodrama again and again (and *again*), and while I admire him for his efforts to undermine traditional narrative tyranny with humor rather than resorting to a Barth-style hatchet job, all four of his novels offer the same one-dimensional commentary on contemporary U.S. society—a critique that, say, any good Didion essay can chew up and spit out in ten pages. In the end, the fact that a thirty-year writing career hasn't produced a single memorable or even recognizably *human* character strikes me as a pretty damning smear on the career of someone who, at heart, longs to be a humanist.

At any rate, Pynchon does have his admirers, and he also has his followers, or people who are labeled his followers, and they do keep cropping up. I think there's more than a little Pynchon floating around John Kennedy Toole, whose *A Confederacy of Dunces* is a book nearly as bloated as its protagonist; Don DeLillo's social, um, *satires* owe more than a little to Pynchon's work; and in a recent essay in *Harper's* magazine (more on that later) the young novelist Jonathan Franzen declares Pynchon a personal hero. But what these writers seem to be expressing is admiration for an older figure; our subject, David Foster Wallace, moves beyond admiration to adulation—if not, to put it more plainly, outright imitation. Make no mistake: if Wallace's writing is indeed produced in Pynchon's shadow—and he certainly hasn't denied the influence—then it's a virtuosic performance that has eclipsed its progenitor. In short, Wallace out-Pynchons Pynchon, and his third book, *Infinite Jest*, may well be the first novel to out–*Gravity's Rainbow Gravity's Rainbow*.

If nothing else, the success of *Infinite Jest* is proof that the Great American Hype Machine can still work wonders: it wasn't too hard to find someone at Little, Brown to tell me that the novel had moved some 60,000 copies, which for any work of literary fiction is spectacular, but for a novel written by a relatively obscure author—a novel that runs to 1,079 pages to boot—is virtually unheard of (as a point of comparison, I've been told that Norman Mailer's equally immense *Oswald's Tale* sold a mere 42,000 copies out of a print run of 120,000). Further, with the notable exception of the *New York Times, Infinite Jest* has racked up a stack of glowing reviews nearly as thick as it is. What makes the book's success even more noteworthy is that it is, in a word, terrible. Other words I might use include bloated, boring, gratuitous, and—perhaps especially—uncontrolled. I would, in fact, go so far as to say that *Infinite Jest* is one of the very few novels for which the phrase "not worth the paper it's printed on" has real meaning in at least an ecological sense; but to resort to such hyperbole would be to fall into the rut that characterizes many reviews of this novel. It seemed to me as I read through *Infinite Jest*'s press packet that most of these reviewers didn't merely want to *like* the novel, they wanted to *write* like it. I think, if I'm not mistaken, that the psychological term for this condition is mass hysteria.

As the preceding paragraph should make clear, I found *Infinite Jest* immensely unsatisfactory, which is a polite way of saying that I hated it. I resent the five weeks of my life I gave over to reading the thing; I resent every endlessly overelaborated gag in the book, like the ten-page riff on why video telephones are unviable, or the dozen pages on the teenager who won all his tennis matches by playing with a pistol held to his head, or the thousands and thousands and *thousands* of words devoted to pharmaceutical trivia on all sorts of mindaltering drugs; and I resent especially the two hundred pages of tinily typed and deliberately pointless endnotes and "errata," 388 in total, which make the novel a two-bookmark experience. In a hoped-for effort at balance, I also slogged my way through Wallace's freshman effort, a novel called *The Broom of the System*, which, at 450 pages, is a relative lightweight next to *Infinite Jest*; nevertheless, what agony the novel saves one in brevity is more than made up for in banality. The only thing even remotely interesting about Wallace's first novel is that it reads like a study for his second. Both novels are set in an imagined United States; both revolve around an emotionally disturbed family full of geniuses, cripples, and money; both feature a man-made wasteland which becomes central to the national imagination (in *The Broom of the System* it's called the Great Ohio Desert, which is why the book is set in Ohio of all places; in *Infinite Jest* it's called the Great Concavity); both, most importantly, work up an elaborate—and elaborately digressive—plot which is deliberately ended as unsatisfactorily as possible. In other words, David Foster Wallace has not merely written (and, I might add, found publishers for) what amounts to an airbrushed handjob of Thomas Pynchon's fiction: he's done it twice.

About the only thing that distinguishes Wallace's second novel from his first is that there's more of it. *The Broom of the System* has one narrative; *Infinite Jest*, on the other hand, has three, each centered around a single character. There is first of all Hal Incandenza, a teenaged tennis prodigy and marijuana addict who during the course of the book plays tennis and gets high a lot, and then stops getting high—that's his plot. Then there's Don Gately, a former housebreaker and narcotics addict who goes straight before the book even opens and merely at-

tempts to stay that way throughout the course of the novel—
that's *his* plot. And then there's Rémy Marathe, the leader of a
group of Quebecois secessionist wheelchair-bound terrorists,
who spends the first two-thirds of the novel having a conversation with another spy—that's a 700-page conversation, folks—
and then kills a couple of people.

That's the plot of the entire novel.

Although one senses that the intermingling of the three
plotlines is meant to create, in modernist jargon, a "frag-
mented" narrative, one reviewer characterized it more accurately as a "rudimentary three-stroke engine," the operative
word being "rudimentary." Of course, these disparate plots do
occur within a larger and supposedly unifying context—or
maybe it's *not* supposed to be unifying, which would answer
more than a few of my questions. *Infinite Jest* is set in a United
States of the near future, possibly a quarter-century hence; it's
impossible to pin down when exactly, because at an unspecified
point between our now and the book's then the traditional
method of numbering years has been replaced by "revenue-
enhancing subsidized time," an advertising ploy in which each
new year is christened "Year of the Whopper," "Year of the
Tucks Medicated Pad," "Year of the Whisper-Quiet Maytag
Dishmaster," etc. (in an act of literary sadism worthy of Joyce,
this list isn't provided until page 223 of the novel, whereupon
the reader discovers that four of the nine years of subsidized
time are sponsored by foods, two by appliances, and two by butt
products, which more or less typifies the level of humor in the
book). There've been a few other changes too: the United
States has used its clout to coerce Mexico and Canada into
forming an alliance called the Organization of North American

Nations for, apparently, no other reason than the chance to use the acronym ONAN, and, as well, a large part of New England—basically everything above Boston—has been ceded to, or forced on, Canada, and renamed the Great Concavity; it now serves as a dumping ground for all sorts of toxic waste produced by the United States. Hence Rémy Marathe's terrorist organization: the Great Concavity borders Quebec, and pollutants leeching from within it are wreaking havoc on the region.

But this is just the context; what is actually meant to unify the book (or, as I suggested earlier, not unify it) is an experimental film called *Infinite Jest* directed by "après-garde" inventor-turned-filmmaker James O. Incandenza. As the name suggests, James is the father of protagonist #1 Hal; once upon a time James too was a tennis prodigy (as was his father before him), and he used the fortune he earned from his inventions to found the Enfield Tennis Academy—or E.T.A., to proffer yet another loaded acronym—where Hal is a student, and then to finance his experiments in film. Enfield is located in Boston, right next to Ennett House Drug and Alcohol Recovery House (which, if you flip forward 900 pages to note 49, you will find the words "Redundancy *sic*"), where protagonist #2 Don Gately works as caretaker, and where, late in the novel, a master copy of the movie *Infinite Jest* is believed to have surfaced, thus leading protagonist #3 Rémy Marathe to pose as a wheelchair-bound recovering drug addict so he can with some difficulty search the rampless facility for the tape. Now, here's the deal with *Infinite Jest*, the movie and not the book (definitely *not* the book): this movie, or "entertainment," as Rémy Marathe calls it, is said to be so compulsively "entertaining" that every-

one who catches even a glimpse of it will become completely
and permanently transfixed and thereafter capable of doing
nothing but watch the movie. They won't eat or get up to use
the toilet; they will even, according to experiments conducted
by Marathe's organization, cut off their own fingers—without
anesthesia—in exchange for the privilege of watching a few
seconds of the film. And herein is *Infinite Jest*'s (the book's)
major theme: the United States has become a culture addicted
to entertainment, and like all addicts we pursue that entertainment to our own detriment.

On the one hand, Wallace's thesis seems self-evident at this
point in history, when the United States has shifted to an economy striated into white-collar and service-oriented jobs, and
its major growth sector is the collapsed "industries" of entertainment and communications technology; on the other hand,
it's more than a little problematic. What's meant to distinguish
Infinite Jest (the book) from various artifacts that precede it is
the conflation of entertainment with drug addiction, and this
notion is, I think, fundamentally flawed. The really insidious
thing about the U.S. entertainment fetish is not that it's *forced*
on us, but that we *choose* to give over so much of our lives to this
crap: we turn on *Baywatch*, we buy tickets to *Eraser*, we christen
Michael Jackson the King of Pop and indulge him in his public
psychosis (except for Jarvis Cocker, bless his heart). If our actions were involuntary—if, say, *Home Improvement* were forced
on us in the same way that the two-minute hate was forced on
the characters of Orwell's *1984*—then we would be living in a
totalitarian society, which as a system is relatively simple to describe (the effects on the people who live under that system are,
of course, not so simple, a fact Orwell recognized, which is why

1984 is a great book and *Infinite Jest* is not). It's more complex than that, I know, but the issue is Wallace's, not mine; still, for him to suggest that free will is involved in the culture of entertainment would essentially eradicate his novel's *raison d'être*. The closest he comes is the unstated implication that, like people who become drug addicts, people who become addicted to entertainment do so because their lives are sad, kind of, and empty, or they had bad childhoods.

Well, duh.

As we say in the East Village, that and $2.50 (not including tip) will buy you a skinny mochaccino.

Lots of great books are built around flawed or at any rate contestable social theories, like *Remembrance of Things Past*, or Mishima's novels, and let's not forget our very own William Faulkner. In fact—and this may merely be a product of my education in deconstruction and identity politics—I take it as a given that the social theories which inform works of fiction *should* be contested by the reader, precisely because they *are* made up; ultimately—and this may be just a product of my education in a more classical formalism—a novel's true merit (or lack thereof) rests on aesthetic considerations. Which is another way of saying that I don't just dislike *Infinite Jest* because I think its premise is simplistic. I think in fact that there's a pretty good satire lurking inside *Infinite Jest*, but it's lost inside about 800 pages of crap.

My reading experience was something like this: for about a hundred pages I was simply lost. I figured this was deliberate on the author's part, and while I dislike that sort of thing on principle I was being paid to read the book, and so I persevered. When enough puzzle pieces had fallen into place—when, eventually, the relatively simple plot of the book took shape and I learned to bracket off Wallace's intentionally unbalancing digressions—I settled in and began to enjoy the book, which, unlike most of Pynchon's writing, is actually engaging on a page-by-page basis. Much has been made of Wallace's method: Sven Birkerts, writing in the *Atlantic Monthly*, called it "idiosyncratic"; Walter Kirn claimed that it has a "certain overall florid nerdiness" in *New York* magazine; in *Elle*, Gerald Howard wrote that "no other writer working communicates so dazzlingly what life will feel like the day after tomorrow"; of course, Gerald Howard just happens to have been Wallace's editor on *The Broom of the System*, but hey.

Of all the comments, the only one I really buy is Birkerts' "idiosyncratic," which is what any good writer's prose should be, and, sentence by sentence, David Foster Wallace is a very good writer indeed. If Pynchon's prose is tentacular, Wallace's prose could be called carnivorous (I was going to say omnivorous, but David Foster Wallace strikes me as a boy who did not eat his vegetables). As a style, it's more than a little infatuated with the jargon of various groups, like homosexuals or drug addicts or teenaged white boys or inner city black people or science nerds: *Infinite Jest* is chock-full of anecdotes about the purveyors of these jargons for what seems no other reason than to give Wallace a chance to write, not just slangily, but with different kinds of slang. There is, I think, an important aesthetic at work in Wallace's prose, and that is the freedom from being good, or, more accurately, the freedom to be bad. Like Pynchon, Wallace's metaphors for certain ideas—like, say, the human condition—are often other ideas—like quantum mechanics— and there's a sort of faux sloppiness about his prose that enables him to discuss with relative fluency (or, often, lack of fluency) all sorts of subjects—Wittgenstein, Descartes, calculus, physics, twelve-step programs, tennis—without resorting to academese. This doesn't mean that Wallace's discursive passages aren't often boring, but it does mean that they're probably a lot less boring than they could be. What it also means is that whenever Wallace's hold on his material is a little shaky, he can hide behind the stutter of an ellipsis or a burst of expletives. It's sort of like a trick I used on history exams: when I couldn't remember the name of a particular general in a battle, I'd merely scribble gibberish in place of a word and hope that my reputation as a good student combined with the professor's laziness would take care of things; more often than not, it worked. As an aesthetic, Wallace's bad (hand)writing has a lot more to do with punk than with Pynchon, which is probably why I like it. I don't think it's merely a way of cheating, or of rendering meaning ambiguous: it can actually be a way to tell the reader things that the writer doesn't know. But as with just about everything else in Wallace's novels, the tendency is so overindulged it was quickly rendered uninteresting, and soon it just became annoying.

But then again, I might just be being generous (I know, I doubt it too). Though I'd like to think that Wallace was actually embracing a sort of epistemological anarchy, it could just be that he's a coward. In an essay on Dostoevsky for the *Voice Literary Supplement*, Wallace departed from his ostensible subject to declare

So, for me anyway, what makes Dostoevsky invaluable is that *he possessed a passion, conviction, and engagement with deep moral issues that we, here, today, cannot or do not allow ourselves* (my italics [i.e., Wallace's]). And on finishing [his biography͡], I think any serious American reader/writer will find himself driven to think hard about what exactly it is that makes so many of the novelists of our own time look so thematically shallow and lightweight, so impoverished in comparison to Gogol, Dostoevsky, even lesser lights like Lermontov and Turgenev. To inquire of ourselves why we—under our own nihilist spell—seem to require of our writers an ironic distance from deep convictions or desperate questions, so that contemporary writers have to either make jokes of profound issues or else try somehow to work them in under cover of some formal trick like intertextual quotation or incongruous juxtaposition, sticking them inside asterisks as part of some surreal, defamiliarization-of-the-reading-experience flourish.[1]

Forced ironic distance? Surreal flourishes? Nihilist *spell*? Aside from the fact that his last sentence is actually a contorted fragment, I haven't seen a novelist project his own anxieties to such self-detriment since Hemingway discussed homosexuals with Gertrude Stein in *A Moveable Feast*. While I agree—to an extent—with Wallace's assertion that a "requirement of textual self-consciousness" is "imposed by postmodernism," I don't buy Wallace's follow-up proposition, namely, that writers from some golden age before ours were "free from certain cultural expectations that constrain our own novelists' freedom to be 'serious.' " It seems to me beside the point to list contemporary writers who are engaging with serious moral themes in their fiction, if for no other reason than that there are just *so many* of them; what strikes me as more useful is a

---

[1] David Foster Wallace, "Feodor's Guide," *VLS*, April 1996, 17.

brief investigation into Wallace's belief that writers today aren't *allowed*—the choice of words is, I think, revelatory— "passion, conviction, and engagement" with deep moral issues.

And so we return to that essay in *Harper's* magazine I mentioned at the start of this review, the one by Jonathan Franzen. By way of introduction I'll only say that Franzen does in fact manage to project his own anxieties to greater detriment than either Hemingway or Wallace—who, by the way, is a friend of Franzen's and a contributing editor at *Harper's*. The ostensible subject of Franzen's essay is his "despair about the American novel," but what it quickly reveals itself to be about is his contempt for what another of his idols, Don DeLillo, has called "around-the-house-and-in-the-yard" fiction, and what that is, in case you're wondering, is fiction that seems to be about *people* as opposed to *ideas*. The opposition is ludicrous; but what's more pertinent here is Franzen's projection of these "people"— and their creators—as being almost universally *not* white, *not* straight, and *not* male—in other words, *not like him*. And what, finally, should Franzen use to make his point than a letter from his friend, David Foster Wallace:

> A contemporary culture of mass-marketed image and atomized self-interest is going to be one without any real sort of felt community. Just about everybody with any sensitivity feels like there's a party going on that they haven't been invited to—we're *all* alienated. I think the guys who write directly about and *at* the present culture tend to be writers who find their artistic invalidation especially painful. I mean it's not just something to bitch about at wine-and-cheese parties: it really *hurts* them. It makes them *angry*. And it's

> not an accident that so many of the writers "in the shadows"
> are straight white males. Tribal writers can feel the loneli-
> ness and anger and identify themselves with their subcul-
> ture and can write to and for their subculture about how the
> mainstream culture's alienated them. White males *are* the
> mainstream culture." [2]

It's not all that often that I'm tempted to trot out the O-word,
but along about the time Wallace refers to everyone from Toni
Morrison to Salman Rushdie to me as "tribal writers," I find
myself getting offended. Wallace's letter is rife with contradictions, but the chief one is this: on the one hand "we're *all* alien-
ated" (his italics, not mine); on the other, there seem to be a
bunch of "tribal writers" excluded from Wallace's notion of
"we"—not to mention from his notion of "sensitivity"—who
seem to be living it up with our "subcultures" at wine-and-
cheese parties he's not invited to. If Wallace's statement
amounts to anything more than a (sadly) fashionably anti–p.c.
complaint about his loss of straight white male privilege, I
don't see it; and, given the list of awards he trumpets on his *Infinite Jest* bio, not to mention the reported $75,000 advance he
received for the novel, let's not even *talk* about "artistic invalidation." Gore Vidal, who's sucked more than a few dicks in his
life *and* been taken to task for it, has written far more persua-
sively that the novel as forum—as opposed to form—has become essentially a cultural irrelevance, but you don't ever hear
him whinging about "artistic invalidation."
  I'm going to close on that note, rather deliberately hastily,

---

[2] Jonathan Franzen, "Perchance to Dream," *Harper's*, April 1996, 51.

with a few lines from Susan Sontag's "Notes on 'Camp' ":
"Without *passion* [my italics], one gets pseudo-Camp—what is
merely decorative, safe, in a word, chic. On the barren edge of
Camp lie a number of attractive things: the sleek fantasies of
Dalí, the Haute couture preciosity of Albicocco's *The Girl with
the Golden Eyes . . .* "[3] and to that list I would add the writing of
Thomas Pynchon and David Foster Wallace. If I cared about
such things—and, in general, I do not—I could, à la Edward
Said, accuse Wallace of cultural colonialism in the peppering of
his otherwise exclusively white-male text with exoticized
African Americans, women, and homosexuals; and, further, I
think that a case can be made that the narrative technique Wallace has derived from Pynchon is nothing more than a watered-
down, de-(homo)eroticized style that lives on Sontag's "barren
edge of Camp." All of which, I suppose, is just a polite way of
saying that if the author of *Infinite Jest* maybe shut off his god-
damn word processor and tried to find someone who would
passionately shove a dick up his ass he might realize, first of all,
that life is just as tough down at the wine-and-cheese party,
and, secondly, that the human mind will in fact force most actions into some sort of satisfactory narrative form. The end of
the *book*, in other words, is not necessarily the end of the *story*,
and by the way: in gay bars, we call this sort of thing "reading,"
and David Foster Wallace, you can now sleep easy, because you
have just been *read*.

---

[3] Susan Sontag, "Notes on 'Camp' " in *Against Interpretation* (New York: Far-
rar Straus and Giroux, 1961), 285.

3

Stop Thinking: The (D)evolution of Gay Literature

Flesh and Blood by Michael Cunningham
The Facts of Life by Patrick Gale
How Long Has This Been Going On? by Ethan Mordden
Like People in History by Felice Picano

1.

At some point early in the AIDS epidemic—this would have been around 1983, a time when no gay man in the United States knew when or even if he would fall ill with the complex of maladies that had begun killing gay men in 1981, a time when HIV had not yet been discovered, let alone its modes of transmission or prophylaxis, a time when government funding for research into these mysteries was minimal and education and support services were virtually nonexistent, a time when, as well, most gay men seemed to regard the rallies and protests and clandestine gatherings of the fifties and sixties as logically capped by the disco-circuit hedonism of the seventies, and a time when many of those men still seemed to view any attack on that hedonism as the ultimate affront to their political and personal freedom—Larry Kramer remarked that just staying alive had become a political act for gay men.

A few years before the plague appeared, in 1978, Kramer had ridden to prominence—and controversy—on the new wave of gay literature with his novel *Faggots*. Fiction with homosexual content had trickled out through the century, from Thomas Mann's *Death in Venice* to Gore Vidal's *The City and the Pillar* to the work of Genet and Isherwood and Baldwin and Burroughs, but as each new book or play or poem appeared it was isolated and treated as a one-off; if the work was regarded as a critical success it was despite its homosexual content, if the work failed it was because of it. But by the 1970s gay men in the United States had attached themselves, like Latinos, blacks, and Jews before them, to a politicized monolithic notion of community, and as part of their newly minted solidarity they wanted the trappings that come with it: political clout, places to live and socialize without fear, and—the endeavor which has so far proved most successful—cultural artifacts to record their place in history. Gay men, in short, wanted their own art, and the easiest, cheapest, and most accessible form of art has always been the written word. By the mid-seventies an organization called the Violet Quill had formed, and its members, Robert Ferro, Michael Grumley, Andrew Holleran, Felice Picano, Edmund White, and George Whitmore, together with film critic Vito Russo and editor and academic George Stambolian, began producing books whose examination of gay life, though sometimes programmatic, was still infused with the raw brashness of tongues only recently untied. Certainly the Violet Quill's members weren't responsible for all gay writing produced in the seventies, but the group does seem a remarkably fortuitous meeting of minds, and is often portrayed as a latter-day gay version of Bloomsbury or the Beat circle of Kerouac and Ginsberg and Burroughs—a group, in other words, whose romanticized reputation, like the Beats and Modernists before it, frequently overshadows its writing. That such talent just happened to gather in a New York City apartment once a week is said to stand as a testament, then and now, to the burgeoning power of the gay story itself, bursting to be told.

In the midst of all this celebration, Kramer's *Faggots* had fallen like the apple of discord. Years later—around the same time he referred to gay men's survival as a political act—Kramer would claim that he had meant his novel's criticisms in a light-hearted, even loving manner, but even a cursory reading of *Faggots* reveals that the actual attitude is closer to despair, a despair not infrequently tinged with contempt. To Kramer, the relentless pursuit of sex and drugs and the ultimate party wasn't merely immature but unhealthy, both psychologically and physically, and if such a message was unpopular, it nevertheless sold well: *Faggots* became a bestseller even as its author was vilified throughout the gay press. It didn't help Kramer's reputation when, three years after its original publication, *Faggots* was proved not merely an accurate description of its own era, but, in its prediction of an ever-growing tide of sexually transmitted disease, a prophetic account of what was to come, and Larry Kramer once again climbed on a soapbox, this time in defense of gay men's lives.

It's been twenty years since that early wave of gay fiction

began appearing, classics like Andrew Holleran's *Dancer from the Dance,* George Whitmore's *Nebraska,* Edmund White's *Nocturnes for the King of Naples;* and it's been a decade since the first AIDS fiction started to show up, Robert Ferro's *Second Son,* David B. Feinberg's *Eighty-Sixed,* Allen Barnett's beautiful *The Body and Its Dangers.* Today, thanks to both political pressure and recognition of the growing gay market, gay sections can be found in most of the chain bookshops, and independent gay bookstores can be found in most major cities. Their shelves are packed with fiction about gay and lesbian life: in two decades, a few dozen books have become many thousands, so many that the single genre of gay literature has now become many sub-genres: in fiction alone there are children's stories, books written for juveniles, coming out narratives, mysteries, erotica, and AIDS stories, as well as the generic label of "fiction" for those books which can't be placed in a single category—and all of these categories are, of course, further divided by gender and race.

The newest category of fiction to squeeze onto already overcrowded shelves is the gay male epic. The word *epic* casts a wide net, though here the primary claim to epicdom seems to be not depth of thought but depth-of-book, measured not in pages but inches. This is territory originally carved out—well, not carved exactly, more like landscaped—by *Gone with the Wind,* and promulgated by everyone from Jacqueline *Valley of the Dolls* Susann to Larry *Terms of Endearment* McMurtry. You know the books I mean. If you don't actually read them you've at least seen them on the subway, mostly carried by women in secretarial or nursing or waitress uniforms staring intently at incredibly thick tomes with gilt covers, embossed lettering, and heavily retouched photographs of busty women in the arms of Fabio. It's interesting—at any rate, I think it's meant to be interesting—that gay male writers are appropriating a form which over the past half century has become an almost exclusively female domain, books written by women, about women, and aimed at that segment of the female population which buys a book at the supermarket along with creamed corn and instant potatoes. I think that this is, in part, meant to be campy, if not in content then in form, a transformative elevation that raises the gaudy to the glamorous in the same way that a tacky dress—sequined, frilled, ribboned, and cut real low—becomes stunning, simply stunning darling, when a man puts it on.

But a tacky dress is a tacky dress is a tacky dress, and what elevates some drags to the status of divas while others remain mere queens is the quality of performance. In other words, the dress isn't as important as what you do once you've got it on. Thus, gay epics, just like their straight counterparts, tend to be multigenerational sagas sometimes focusing on a single individual, sometimes on a family, but in either case spanning decades meticulously marked out by hairdos, clothing styles, brand names, period slang, and, whenever possible, major historical events. But unlike contemporary pulp epics, gay epics are written with a political mission: to insert gay people into times and places where their existence was previously minimized and distorted, if not denied. In other words, a quarter century after Stonewall, gay writers are still trying to script themselves into history. *Almost History, Like People in History, American Studies:* the titles of these three recent gay epics, as well as Larry Kramer's long-awaited *The American People,* make this explicit right up front; *Flesh and Blood, The Facts of Life*, and *How Long Has This Been Going On?* also manage to suggest a grand historical aspect on their covers. But the question remains: why put the dress on in the first place?

Before I answer that question, I have a confession to make, or at least a clarification of my position: I was raised on trashy books. I grew up in rural Kansas; the nearest library was twenty miles from my house, and, especially in the summer, the only books around were my stepmother's and the ones my older sister had procured through school catalogs. At my high school, Daphne du Maurier was on the English department reading list, along with Taylor Caldwell and all those other books by Twain. I read Sidney Sheldon's first five novels, Judith Krantz's first three; until I went to college I believed *Watership Down* was the best book I ever read—and I was right. What attracted me then, though I didn't realize it until years after I stopped reading epics, wasn't the strength of the narrative, but its length: the only thing better than V.C. Andrews' *Flowers in the Attic* was its sequel, *If There Be Thorns* (or it might have been *Petals on the Wind,* I forget the order). Some books resort to gimmicks like suspense or humor or interesting characters to keep you reading, but readers of epics keep turning pages for the simple reason that they *can.* The end of the story isn't merely postponed in a true epic: it is, in some fundamental way, denied. Even if the author dies the books can go on, as witnessed by 1992's *Scarlett: The Sequel to Margaret Mitchell's Gone with the Wind* by Alexandra Ripley, then the fastest-selling American novel of all time. This last is, I think, the telling detail. In denying that the story ever ends, the epic denies also that the Real Story—to put it bluntly, life—will come to an end, and for a population looking to replace a god it doesn't really believe in but unable to get their insurance to cover a therapist, a $4.95 paperback helps fill the gap. Think of Kathy Bates in *Misery*, breaking James Caan's ankles, tying him to a desk, forcing him to resurrect in one novel the character he had killed in another. Bates is crazy but recognizable, the fan turned back into fanatic, whose only desire is to *keep on reading*.

AIDS—to bring us back to gay epics—is the specific manifestation of the narrative-ending force in gay life, and, now, in much of its literature. But in an epic beginning in the thirties or forties or fifties, the epidemic of the past fifteen years occupies only a tiny place—a place which most of these books tend to diminish even more. In this way AIDS is contextualized, its threat minimized. To put it another way, the (wo)man in the dress is tied to a railroad track whose chugging narrative locomotive will charge right through the flimsy obstacle and keep on going. This is the reason, then, why gay male writers are putting on their tacky dress: to destroy it, and the part of themselves that wants to put it on.

2.

Perhaps the first gay epic was Armistead Maupin's *Tales of the City*. At seven volumes and published over a twenty-year span, it's as long as all the other gay epics combined, and it has proved enormously popular as well, even spawning a mini-series in England. *Tales of the City* has always struck me as one long bar story punctuated by mildly ribald humor, a drunkard's Proust if you will; nevertheless it remains the best-selling gay title ever. Then there's Edmund White's idiosyncratic and autobiographical trilogy whose first volume, *A Boy's Own Story*, was set in the fifties, continued through the sixties in *The Beautiful Room Is Empty*, and is set to deal with post-Stonewall and post-AIDS gay life in *The Farewell Symphony*, due out sometime in 1996. White's writing in the first two books has moved away from the pure lyricism of his early fiction to a sort of cool luminous reportage that reminds one of the work of our more storied essayists, Joan Didion or John McPhee, and one expects that the final volume of his trilogy will be in this vein. Maupin and White began their multivolume sagas more than a decade ago, but in the past few years the number of these big books has increased rapidly: in 1994, Christopher Bram published his Washington, D.C., tale, *Almost History*; in 1995, Laura Argiri's nineteenth-century melodrama *The God in Flight* came out, along with Mark Merlis' study of McCarthyism in academia, *American Studies*; 1996 has seen the publication of four epics: Michael Cunningham's *Flesh and Blood*, Patrick Gale's *The Facts of Life*, Ethan Mordden's *How Long Has This Been Going On?*, and Felice Picano's *Like People in History*.

The cover line for Picano's novel, "a gay American epic," recalls the subtitle of Tony Kushner's *Angels in America*, "a gay fantasia on national themes," and the title of the novel is taken from an unpublished book by Edmund White. In fact, everything about *Like People in History* hints at something else, humor, suspense, politics, drama, and especially, as the title suggests, history, but in the end all these suggestions don't combine to make anything except for a tediously elaborated narrative. This story is split into two interwoven parts: one very long night in 1991—a birthday party, an AIDS demonstration, a stint in jail, a midnight quarrel in Central Park, an attempted suicide, a fistfight, an ambulance ride, a fallen crane, a traffic pileup, and, finally, a death—and the thirty-six years of acquaintance between Roger Sansarc, the novel's narrator, and his cousin Alistair Dodge, which lead up to that night. Picano's story pauses in 1954, 1961, 1969, 1974, 1979, and 1985; these pauses are meant to reveal not just significant moments in the lives of the characters—two gay white upper-middle-class men—but significant moments in the history of America and, in particular, of that segment of the American gay community to which Roger and Alistair belong: the A-list (for clarification, see Ethan Mordden below).

The novel's single sustained conflict is presented in the opening pages—will Roger, who is HIV-negative, help Alistair, who has AIDS, kill himself?—and isn't resolved until the book's final scene. A potent situation, but as the novel unfolds it becomes increasingly uninteresting, not just because Alistair is a complete shit to everyone around him, but because he is, above all, a complete shit to Roger. Puppylike, Roger keeps coming back to Alistair, but each time a chance comes for Picano to demonstrate or explain *why* pious Roger is attracted to boorish Alistair, he ducks his responsibility. Take, for example, 1974's scene, when Roger reveals that he has re-befriended Alistair after a scene in 1969 in which—take a deep breath—Alistair persuades a leftist gay dentist to mistreat an abscessed tooth in Roger's mouth shortly before Roger is subjected to his Selective Service medical examination, thus causing Roger to lose consciousness at the exam on the same day as dozens of similarly mistreated dupes around the country collapse at various draft boards and by their collective swoon manage to embarrass the government into changing the Selective Service guidelines and produce a more equitable system. Now—you may breathe again—five years later, Roger's only comment is "I'd forgiven him for the Selective Service madness. Forgiven him, and moved to his elected city." That's it. No explanation, no fallout, not even a dental retainer: just Social Change and a change of address. This sort of thing happens so often that one wonders not if Roger will assist in Alistair's suicide, but why he hasn't killed him already.

The answer, of course, is that Alistair's misdeeds aren't interesting enough to merit murder. Typically, an epic's antagonist is more compelling than its protagonist in his or her evil grotesquerie—think, in TV terms, of J.R. Ewing and Alexis Carrington, or, for that matter, of Satan in *Paradise Lost*—but Alistair is blandly bad and slightly silly; at his worst, he's a lapsed Christian Socialist's bad dream of idleness and insensitivity. In other words, Tony Blair would hate him. As a foil to this, Roger comes across as, well, a lapsed Christian Socialist who also happens to be gay. If Alistair is a bland villain, Roger is a boring hero, a character invested with an almost Randian sense of self-righteousness. Roger hands out bread and apples to the starving masses at Woodstock; Roger's lover Matt is voted the sexiest gay man in America *twice*; Roger edits the most influential gay magazine in the country; Roger's celebrated history of gay life is adapted into a critically acclaimed play. In his account of the shining moments of Roger's life, Picano tries to elevate a soapbox into the magic mountain, but he never realizes that he goes over the top too early, and as a result his novel spends most of its time tumbling head over heels. Rock bottom comes abruptly, when Roger meets his dying lover's parents for the first time. His parents, Matt had barely managed to gasp, are "sim . . . ple . . . peo . . . ple," but it's not until Roger meets them that we discover "sim . . . ple" is Matt's euphemism for Down syndrome, and what follows is an unbearably maudlin scene in which Roger tells "Papa" and "Mama" that the two-time winner of Mr. Gay America is dying. The threesome have an extended conversation on homosexuality, AIDS, and the myth of Achilles and Patroclus, all conducted in a five-year-old's English, which seems to be a sort of lowest-common-denominator approach to both narrative and morality. In a book already groaning with gimmicks, it is—barring The Cure—the last trick Picano could pull from his bag, but it backfires, because the words and ideas Matt's retarded parents use are no less sophisticated than those used anywhere else in *Like People in History*. The scene finally pulls off the novel's mask of false naivete and forced melodrama and reveals something which is—in the language of Papa and Mama—boring, plain and simple.

The storyline of Ethan Mordden's *How Long Has This Been Going On?* is eerily similar to that of *Like People in History*. The book spans the years 1949 to 1991, almost exactly the same dates as Picano's novel, and though the particulars of Mordden's narrative are distinct from Picano's, its generalities are all the same. There are the fifties, in which men (and, in this case, a few women) struggle to accept their homosexuality; there are the pot-smokin' hip-shakin' drug-takin' sixties; there is Stonewall and disco in the seventies; there is AIDS and backlash in the eighties; and there is, in the end, the hint of triumph promised by the nineties. *How Long*'s chief distinction from *Like People in History*—besides a generally higher standard of prose, as well as a comical touch that is actually if only occasionally funny—is that its narrative is incident- rather than plot-driven. At first I found this refreshing, since, in Picano's case, dropping the engine of a thriller into the body of a polemic produced a rant that got nowhere fast. But *How Long*'s extreme length—just under 600 pages—calls out for some sort of form which never materializes. The novel proceeds at a pace that is both lazy and erratic; its nameless, faceless narrator glosses over scenes that merit sharp inspection and devotes paragraphs to details which are trivial rather than illustrative. Reading the book was a bit like channel surfing, but the remote was in someone else's hand.

In lieu of a plot, *How Long* offers protagonists. There is Lois, the butch dyke who runs a gay club; Elaine, the femme who leaves her husband for Lois and becomes a noted author; Johnny the Kid, aka Johnny Smith, aka Jerrit Troy, aka the Green Goddess, the lounge singer at Lois' club who, in donning a dress, seemingly *invents* camp; Larkin, the nervous member of an early gay group, so nice that he'll always be someone's boyfriend, so bland that he'll always be left behind; Frank, the son who leaves his father, the cop who leaves the force, and the man who first leaves Larkin behind; Blue, the hustler everybody wants who becomes a traveling AIDS activist and so earns a place in heaven somewhere between the archangel Gideon and Johnny Appleseed; Luke, the man who loves the man who hates to loves him; Tom, the man who is loved by the man who hates to love him; Walt, the cousin of the man who is loved by the man who . . . ; and Claude, Walt's teddy bear. And there are more characters, so many that there are often more characters on the page than there are things for them to do.

When, however, the stories of one set of characters run out of steam, Mordden just throws a few more into the mix. In a book about the diversity of gay life, this was, I assume, intentional, and it could have been effective—the dozens of characters in *Anna Karenina*, after all, are drawn from only a tiny segment of Russian society—but Mordden's characters are, on the one hand, not diverse, and, on the other, not compelling. They're simply ciphers demarcated by gender, skin color, age, Stepford Wives whose sole function is to show that being a gay man or lesbian is a tough job, but with a little programming anyone can do it.

The reason why Mordden's characters are automatons— and, as well, why his novel lacks a plot—is because, among all his characters, not one of them is the Bad Guy. Picano, with Alistair, makes an effort at creating a villain, but Mordden's aim is, in a way, more pure. His book's only antagonist—and the true antagonist of Picano's novel, the force which makes Alistair bad—is Society. Specifically, straight society, that amorphous mass composed of ninety percent of the population which seems to exist solely to make life as difficult as possible for the gay ten percent. The idea that one's "identity"—be it ethnic, religious, sexual, or otherwise—places one in perpetual conflict with a more powerful other is a classic American trope in both politics and literature, and as it happens the particular sentiment which informs Picano and Mordden's stories is not one with which I disagree. But a novel which aspires to social criticism ought to depict the society it criticizes. There are plenty of wonderful novels about gay life almost completely devoid of straight people, but if, as a novelist, exposing homophobia is your mission, then it seems worthwhile to point out that

there's only so much one can learn about homophobia by looking at gay people; eventually you have to examine the homo-
phobes, and that means looking at straight people. Think of the
interaction between Jews and Gentiles in Saul Bellow, between
blacks and whites in Toni Morrison; think, as well, of the criticism of their own communities a Morrison or a Bellow novel is
sure to provide, a quality completely absent in these two books.
Mordden, like Picano, gives straight folk short shrift, opting
for an occasional tinny caricature of someone's parents—who
either don't accept or just don't understand their child's homosexuality—or of a serial murderer of gay men, or of a group of
gas mask–wearing bashers attacking a gay-pride parade. As a
result Mordden's characters are reduced to wailing and flail-
ing their way through an Us-Against-Them world in which
They are unusually absent. As a strategy, it seems a bit like
playing racquetball in a court with no walls, and that same
image could describe the progress of Mordden's narrative:
each scene gets one good *whack*, and then it rolls off into the
distance.

The bad guy, then, is an evil specter; what conflicts do appear—Will I Ever Fall In Love? Am I Making The Right Career Choice? Should I Move To San Francisco?—are, like the
conflicts in a sitcom, predictably easy to resolve, and what's left
to drag the reader forward are Mordden's frequent pronouncements of his grand theme: that his characters, and gay people in
general, have an important role to play in history. When, for
example, über–gay man Frank announces that yes, he will
come to San Francisco, Mordden writes, "Indeed, Frank was
coming: because destiny wanted him to. Frank has a date with
his future, which needs him in a certain place some years from

now, to save the life of someone he has never heard of, a young man named Lonnie Ironwood. Some of us float, some of us make choices, and a very few of us, like Frank, are Summoned." Comments like this appear regularly. Rather than kindle interest in a developing story, all they really do is indicate the author's fundamental lack of faith in it, and therein lies the flaw at the core of both Mordden and Picano's books: they are not "protest novels"—a dismissive term applied to books as diverse and literary as *Huckleberry Finn, Native Son,* and *Portnoy's Complaint*—as much as they are novels which protest too much, declaring in this case not innocence but importance.

Many of Mordden's protests come from Elaine, who, in her struggle to include lesbian content in her fiction, is quickly revealed to be Mordden's stand-in crusader. "It's not my job as a writer to make you happy," Elaine declares early on. "It's my job to make you think." What she wants you to think is this: "It's a world with entirely new rules." This statement, made about a gay bar, is soon extended to the entire gay milieu, a "new world" built of bars called Hero's and peopled with men who are sexually ranked A, B, "borderline," "I-don't-know," and D—the "total rejects" (the alphabet, it seems, is also being reinvented). In Mordden's world, and Picano's as well, gay men— and lesbians too!—have broken from the bonds of history. Stand up, straight people, and take note: paradise is as easy as a gym membership, a disco beat, and a bottle of poppers. Elaine: "I shall advise you . . . That's precisely why we obviously contented and self-respecting old lezbies and queens are here." Again, Elaine: "the boys struck her as pioneers, experimenting in the creation of a culture." And again Elaine, talking with her editor Johnna:

"It's hard to believe," says Elaine, "that there was a time when such people had nothing of their own to go to but dingy demimonde saloons. Now they're dating and dancing like teenagers in July."

"Yes, it's been a reestablishing decade," Johnna responds. Her hand explains, vaguely. "Diversities."

"Will our lit reflect those diversities, I wonder?" A loaded question.

Johnna smiles. "Your book."

"My book and other books. Other writers' books."

A loaded question indeed. This is Ethan Mordden at his worst, grabbing his doggerel by the bone and shaking it with gleeful ferocity until it's dead, but the truth is that Mordden never delivers anything that looks like a new world, a new culture, a new code of behavior. Occasionally he shows us people trying to live their lives, and that, one would have thought, would be enough to fill any book. But: "I don't do small talk," is one character's fatalistic pronouncement. "I only do topics." File under: Epic, Gay (and Lesbian).

When Sally meets Edward in Patrick Gale's *The Facts of Life*, World War II has just ended. Edward's German, Jewish, tubercular, a composer; Sally's his doctor in the East Anglian hospital where he's ended up after ten years as a refugee in England. Courtship is made difficult by her parents' anti-Semitism and the jealousy of Thomas, his male guardian, which seems—and is later confirmed—to be a sexual jealousy; nevertheless, Sally and Edward eventually marry and set up house in The Roundel, the matriarchal home of one Dr. Pertwee, pioneering feminist, sex educator, and Sally's mentor, who bequeaths to her the ramshackle mansion and then retires to a nunnery to die. Sally's past—her mother, cancerous; her father, crippled; and her career in medicine—disappear in the wake of marriage and pregnancy, but Edward's past comes back to haunt him. His parents' deaths in a concentration camp had long been confirmed, but the whereabouts of his sister Miriam remained a mystery. Shortly after his wedding, she is found in an asylum in France. There are scars on her head: she has been experimented on. She is hugely fat, immobile, unresponsive, a vegetable with open eyes. Edward smothers her with a pillow, and when, at one point, he begins to pull back, Miriam helps him to push, offering an absolution which Edward never fully accepts. He suffers a breakdown, attempts to smother his daughter, whom Sally has insisted on naming Miriam, then attempts suicide. In an asylum he undergoes electroshock therapy until Sally spirits him to The Roundel, where, under her care, he recovers. In the ensuing months he has a brief fling with Myra Toye, a film star at the studio where Edward writes Oscar-winning scores, and then, suddenly, Sally dies in a flash flood. Part One ends not here, with Sally hanging like laundry from the limbs of the tree into which the flood has washed her, but at her funeral, where Thomas, Edward's gay guardian, schemes to get Edward back into his house, but settles, in the short term, for the sexy cabbie who had driven him to the funeral.

Patrick Gale's prose moves through *The Facts of Life* like the current of a manicured river, smooth, inexorable, virtually undisturbed by the grand and shabby vessels which travel on its surface, ignorant of whatever palaces or shacks line its shore. For a novel of this length, such prose is something of a saving grace—and it is mercifully free of the political pronouncements that haunt Picano's and Mordden's work—but in the end, I think, such evenhandedness proves Gale's undoing. Courtship, murder, childbirth, insanity: all are described in the same level voice. Every scene, no matter how important or trivial, seems to merit about twenty pages of clean careful observation. By the end of the first half of the novel I found myself confused and slightly uneasy, not by the events of the story, but how to feel about them. Gale seems to rely on some standard array of emotional responses—when someone dies you feel sad, when someone is born you feel happy—and then, the scene's action concluded, he moves on to the next, and, inevitably, the next. And so:

In Part Two, Edward's grandchildren, straight Alison and gay Jamie, are aspiring yuppies; their mother is hippie-turned-bourgeois Miriam, their fathers any of several candidates known collectively as the Beards, men with whom Miriam shared a commune in the sixties. Alison is rescued from an attempted rape by Sam, a mysterious and sexy builder who moves in with her but soon ends up with Jamie, despite the fact that he's "not queer." It is Jamie's first relationship after hundreds of one-night stands, and it turns out to be his last as well: a routine medical evaluation reveals that he is HIV-positive; within months he's ill, and, eschewing treatment, he's dead within a year. He is brought to The Roundel to die, cared for by Sam, Miriam, Alison, and Edward. Miriam's past as a weak, ineffective mother is atoned for, but Edward proves inflexibly homophobic, and seems only to accept Jamie and Sam's relationship when Sam confesses to Edward that Jamie had asked Sam to kill him, an "act of love" which Sam couldn't perform. The extended deathbed scene which dominates the second half of the book is punctuated by a press scandal concerning Myra and Edward, whose fling, apparently, blossomed into a long affair in the years between Part One and Part Two; and by Alison's volunteer work at an underfunded AIDS hotline. When, finally, Jamie dies, these two subplots converge with the main: The Roundel is transformed into a retreat for people with AIDS and their caregivers, a charitable organization given chic status by retired soap queen Myra and world-famous composer Edward, who seem bound for romance in their golden years. To complete the picture, Alison, who will run the retreat, is pregnant by Sam, who will stay on as handyman, making sure windows open, doors close, and gutters never clog.

Most novels tell you what they're up to, and most, if you look hard enough, make excuses for themselves; usually, both of these statements are made at the same time. As Alison becomes immersed in caring for Jamie, she "learned the true value of fictive escapism"; at Jamie's insistence, she and Sam attend a "dazzlingly inane musical revival, with a candy-floss love story, lines of chorines stamping gold-spangled tap shoes and astonishingly mobile sets. . . . The undisputed escapism was just what they both needed, enabling them to laugh and smile at nothing in particular, to stop thinking, in fact, for two merciful hours." "Undisputed," I think, is the revelatory word here: truly escapist theater doesn't allow for such postmodern defensive positioning. *The Facts of Life* is, to adapt Gale's phrase, disputed escapism. Though a strong sentiment abounds that all of this should Mean Something—this is the Holocaust, after all, this is the AIDS epidemic—ultimately this novel is merely the flip side of the musical Alison and Sam attend. It's a two-hanky weeper in which tragedy isn't created on the page but borrowed from the sorrows of the reader's own life, and is always, ultimately, pushed away by a continuing narrative: thus Part One closes not with Sally's death but with Thomas scoring the cabbie at her funeral, and Part Two not with Jamie's death but with the slightly silly reincarnation of The Roundel and Edward and Myra's love affair. The entire narrative is too clean, and too cleanly told, for complex emotions to break through Gale's web of words to the reader. This isn't a flaw as much as it's a limitation: in fact, Gale writes with a facility that is almost virtuosic. One critic, commenting on *Schindler's List*, remarked that it took a Steven Spielberg to make a feel-good movie about the Holocaust. Gale has managed to do the same thing with AIDS.

Tragedy isn't Michael Cunningham's objective either. His subject in *Flesh and Blood* is, rather, want, the gap between what one needs and what one has. It seems a modest goal for a novel so grand in scope—but modesty, as Eve Harrington proved, is often the best way to conceal a deeply ambitious nature. In Cunningham's case the mask is benign, almost palliative, a postmodern defense against a contemporary readership conditioned to avoid big themes. Cunningham's book—a book about race, gender, sexuality, class, and all the other de-ismed isms of the post-p.c. world—asserts that want is the one thing that binds humanity together, and it's the tension between that spiritual bond and the almost arbitrary bond of family—the flesh and blood of the title—that gives the novel its conflict.

The opening chapter of *Flesh and Blood* is set in 1935, the penultimate in 1995, but the last two pages take place in 2035. Its century-long span strikes me as a tiny nod to Gabriel García Márquez's *One Hundred Years of Solitude*. There are others: both novels concern several generations of a single family, both, in ways as different as the cultures that produced them, trace their family's fortunes against a backdrop of social rather than political history, and both depict characters whose personalities and personal fortunes are almost brutally unchanging. García Márquez is called a magical realist, Cunningham's realism is psychological in nature, but though they look through different lenses, both authors seem to see human nature as a slave to fate, whether that fate is imposed from within the self or from without. But, for me, the most resonant similarity is one of voice. García Márquez once remarked that he was unable to create successful fiction until he learned to write in the voice his grandmother had used to tell him stories; and *Flesh and Blood* is full of matriarchal references: to Madame Bovary, to Anna Karenina, to *Middlemarch*. Cunningham's aunts may well be pulp-epic novelists like Judith Krantz and Barbara Taylor Bradford, but his true literary mothers are the great novelists of the eighteenth and nineteenth centuries: Austen, all three Brontës, and—I am thinking in terms of her strict moral vision—Eliot.

Cunningham's novel traces four generations of the Stassos family: Constantine, its old-world patriarch, is a Greek immigrant to the United States; he marries Mary, an Italian-American girl whose family, like the family she marries into, struggles to call itself part of the middle class. Both are, in their own way, greedy: Constantine wants money, Mary respectability, and, of the two, Constantine proves more successful. A chance conversation in a bar with a fellow Greek sets him up in construction, and over the years he climbs the ladder of wealth.

Mary manages each successively larger home, but no amount of purchased elegance manages to open the doors of her snobby neighbors, and so she attempts to console herself by shoplifting the tiniest, most inexpensive items. Susan, their efficient eldest daughter, is Constantine's too-valued favorite; she escapes from his "kisses and hugs" by marrying an ambitious if stolid Republican and achieving a success that is so dry it's almost desiccated. Will, the middle child, is his mother's favorite; her vision of him carefully excludes his homosexuality, though when he does finally reveal it to her she is shown a lifestyle not much different from her own. It's Zoe, the youngest, who proves most strange to mother and father, prompting Constantine to worry if "he'd made a foreigner's life for her with something as simple as a name." Zoe is born a little too late for the sixties, but she lives the life anyway, a life of carefree sex and drug use; her best friend is a drag queen, her child the son of a black man she dates for only a few months. Time passes; Constantine leaves Mary for Magda, who isn't generous, but is ample, in all the ways Mary had grown stingy and skinny. Jamal, Zoe's son, and Ben, Susan's son, become part of the story; Zoe falls ill with AIDS. It's Zoe's illness that keeps the family members from drifting their separate ways, and it's her death, and Ben's homosexuality, that finally rip it apart. Ben is the model child of a model family, handsome, smart, athletic, kind, above all, *loved*, and his greatest desire is not to lose that love or to hurt those who love him, which he sees as the inevitable result of his homosexuality. These ideas exist just below the surface of Ben's consciousness and are revealed in a code that never uses any taboo words, as is his final decision, which is to commit suicide rather than reveal himself. His death shatters the family and effectively ends the novel, though Cunningham offers a denouement which, like so much else in this novel, is Victorian in origin but feels almost postmodern in spirit. In brief paragraphs, Cunningham traces each of his characters to his death, and if any similarity to the pulp epic remains by the end of his book, he casts it off here: he firmly, finally ends the story he began.

In fact, throughout the course of *Flesh and Blood*, Cunningham is less concerned with the surface events of his narrative—the plot, in other words—than with the way his characters react to changing circumstances. Cunningham's narrative *is* compelling—at times it seems to consume time rather than merely surrender to it—but it is in small circumstances that his pen prefers to linger. Decorating a cake can be revelatory, climbing a tree religious; and every sentence, no matter how mundane its subject, is occasion for a literary event. Such ostentatiousness could go disastrously awry in a less gifted novelist or less perceptive observer, and for much of *Flesh and Blood* I waited uneasily for Cunningham to slip up, but he doesn't: he consistently manages to reveal the general in the particular without resorting to posturing or polemic. Mary "took the brush from Susan and forced it through Zoe's hair so hard that buried thoughts were pulled to the surface of her brain." "Todd's brother's Chevrolet gleamed with everything a new car had to say about freedom and better luck." Constantine "crawled among the gnarls and snags of his father's vineyard, tying errant tendrils back to the stakes with rough brown cord that was to his mind the exact color of righteous doomed effort." What makes these revelations beautiful isn't just their truth, but Cunningham's insistence that all such revelations are idiosyncratic, and even somehow unimportant. This is Zoe, shortly before she dies:

> A bee buzzed onto the porch, hovered over the floorboards. Zoe watched it in its lush, suspended heaviness of body, the transparent shadow it cast. She watched her brother and his lover move together. Was their affection for each other related to the flight of the bee? No, that was just her habit of making connections.

It's a quiet statement, a take-it-or-leave-it declaration about love, about homosexuality, about life and death, and, ultimately, about the use and usefulness of metaphor itself: when you see a bee and its shadow and are reminded of love, when you see a Chevy and think of freedom, you are offered both the ecstasy of possibility and the pain of its absence—of want, of lack. Happiness, Cunningham seems to suggest, only comes when you find a place between the two. Until Ben's death, Constantine is always after more; Mary reconciles herself to less and less; both are unhappy. Of all the characters, Will comes closest to happiness: divorced from his lifelong conflict with his father, and contented with his lover Harry, he becomes joyful and just a bit boring. But it's the kind of boring one feels jealous of—the kind of boring one wants for oneself.

3.

In a better world, *Like People in History* and *How Long Has This Been Going On?* would be published straight into paperback and sold from whirling wire racks at supermarkets; gay men could buy them along with their Evian and sun-dried tomatoes, and their authors would be profiled in some gay version of *Better Homes and Gardens*. To some degree, this is even acknowledged: the jacket copy for *Like People in History* calls it a novel with "all the popular appeal of James Michener, Judith Krantz, and *Forrest Gump*." In fact, the book is as labored as the first, as silly as the second, and as pompous as the third, but—let's face facts—we're still years away from a gay-themed novel that sells on a par with Michener or Krantz. The onus of this second-class status weighs heavily on both Mordden's and Picano's novels; indeed, I would go so far as to claim that it is precisely this sense which ruins them. Good trash revels in its trashiness. Morality isn't so much a theme as the playing field on which the traditional pulp epic unfolds. Rather than make grandiose moral statements, the pulp epic takes for granted the idea of right and wrong and quickly establishes a cast of heroes and villains, and if you removed a few dozen grand pronouncements from either Mordden's or Picano's book, and let the characters have a little more fun, this is precisely the turf you'd be on.

The real problem with these books is not so much their words, but the market those words were written for. By creating an odd and oddly defined category of writing—"gay fiction"—you also create a distinction whose very existence implies a qualitative difference where none exists. As gay fiction has proliferated, the quality of that fiction has tended to vary greatly. This may seem obvious, but in the world of gay books there seems to be a tacit assumption that gay fiction possesses superior aesthetic merit simply for possessing gay content. Time was when there was more than a little truth to this, but nowadays one mostly hears about a writer's "bravery" for including "difficult subject matter" in writing workshops and regional newspapers. Homophobia still exists in the publishing world—only a few years ago I received a rejection letter from the *New Yorker* whose author suggested "psychological difficulties" prevented me from creating "effective fiction"—but the primary obstacle to the success of books with gay themes isn't editors but readers. Straight people still resist picking up books about gay characters, and the ghettoized existence of these books only worsens the situation, implying as it does that these books, and the characters and themes contained in them, *are* different from straight people, outside their experience, beyond their ken. Books such as *Like People in History* and *How Long Has This Been Going On?* seem, on the one hand, to parrot this belief, and, on the other, to disprove it.

Interestingly, this new subgenre of gay epics, which seems designed to bring gay fiction to, if not new heights, then new depth, also contains the possibility of dismantling its parent genre. The form of the contemporary pulp epic has evolved from something that was originally about religion and the state to something that is about people: not individuals but, typically, a family whose members exemplify the various attributes of a single community. In both the United States and here, the most common community represented is the aspiring white middle class, but examples of the genre can be found in black, Jewish, Indian, and other communities. In emphasizing the notion of community, Felice Picano and Ethan Mordden's epics fall right into this category, but in de-emphasizing the family they trap themselves. The members of a community qua members of a community emphasize sameness, but people within families emphasize their differences, and by virtually eliminating the family from their communitarian tracts Mordden and Picano have intentionally or inadvertently gathered together a group of people who all essentially think and act the same way—and the reason for the elimination of the family, one can't help feeling, is that families often contain straight people, and neither Mordden nor Picano wanted to write about them. But the family is an arena in which people attempt to form a personality distinct from the personalities around them; and, in fiction, this provides for a multiplicity of voices and points of view. Both Patrick Gale and Michael Cunningham center their epics on the family, and, in so doing, they're forced to write less about gay people; but by contextualizing homosexuality in this way they manage to say a lot more about both homosexuality and homophobia than either Mordden or Picano. Sam's bisexuality in *The Facts of Life* suggests a more complex view of sexuality than the political dogmatism of *Like People in History* or *How Long Has This Been Going On?* will allow for; Ben's suicide in *Flesh and Blood* is more tragic than any gay-bashing incident in Picano or Mordden's epics, because we see exactly the circumstances that have produced it. Gale is thematically closer to Picano and Mordden than to Cunningham in that he is primarily concerned with using the family to make statements about gay life, albeit much more subtly than Picano and Mordden. Only Cunningham subordinates the topic of homosexuality, using it to comment on the family, rather than the other way around.

Cunningham offers three gay characters: Will, Ben, and Cassandra, Zoe's drag-queen friend. Will's values are that of the liberal middle class, and he has found a life that manages to reflect those values: he's a teacher, he's mostly monogamous, he and Harry take in Jamal after Zoe dies. Ben takes his parents' Republican values and makes them almost stoic in his desire to be loyal to them; because he can't conceive of his homosexuality as anything more than a betrayal to those values, he kills himself. Cassandra is a nurturer: as a boy she raised her younger brothers and sisters in her parents' stead; as an adult she takes care of the teenaged Zoe, and then helps to raise Jamal; she is a former academic, fluent in several languages, a sometime prostitute, a professional shoplifter; she also dies of AIDS. It's Cassandra who, attempting to console Mary about Zoe's illness, suggests waterproof mascara; it's Cassandra who would rather have Jamal go live with Mary than bourgeois Will and Harry after she and Zoe die. The only conflicts she sees between any of her many roles are the conflicts others impose on her; and, as much as possible, she concerns herself with the day-to-day business of living her life according to a code that both acknowledges its conservative roots and tailors it to meet her needs. It is in this last respect that I was reminded of Larry Kramer's remark that just staying alive is a political act for gay men. Kramer was speaking in a post-AIDS context, of course, but I think, in fact, that his sentiment was as true before 1981 as after. The polemical novels of Felice Picano and Ethan Mordden manage to communicate little more than their own posturing. The domestic themes of Patrick Gale and, especially, Michael Cunningham do a far better job of illustrating the tension between society and the self, whether that self is straight or gay, and that, I think, is the ultimate political act for any novel.

4

The Lay of the Land

American Pastoral by Philip Roth

The impulse to read well is, I think, stronger than the impulse to write well. Actually, I'm not sure that there is an impulse to *write* well (as opposed to a generalized desire to excel), but it seems pretty clear that most readers are willing and able to construct complete narratives from even the tiniest snippets of information. This is just as true of lazily written genre fiction as it is of the artful dodging of post-realist writers: a dynamic is created between the limited information the writer can supply—literally, just the words on the page—and the vast breadth of knowledge about how life is lived which the reader brings to those words. Managed properly by both writer and reader, this dynamic can provide for the most sublime reading experience, allowing the reader to become an active agent in the creation of the narrative. I'm thinking here of the obfuscation of the Victorians, especially James; of the essays and novels of Joan Didion, which both forbid and implore the reader to bring his own version of the story to the events at hand; of the seemingly bland fare of Ray Carver's fiction, which is served up in full awareness that the reader will sit down at table with his own salt and pepper.

It is not, however, a technique I associate with Philip Roth. Roth's preferred method has been to bombard the reader with sensory and intellectual stimuli, a gouache painted so stridently that at times it seems held in place by nothing but the muscularity of the stroke; and *American Pastoral*, Roth's twenty-second book and his twenty-first novel (he debuted famously with a collection of stories, *Goodbye, Columbus*, but has rarely allowed himself to be constrained by the form since), seems at first to partake of this method. Nevertheless, this new novel could not survive without an enormous effort of goodwill on the part of its readers. It's not that Roth's method has failed him here; rather, he has failed his method. His tale is not told but recounted, not felt but described; the first three-quarters of this 423-page book are characterized by a near-absolute reliance on summary storytelling—*this* happened then *this* happened then *this* happened then *this* happened—and in lieu of Joycean epiphanies or Woolfian moments of being, readers are offered an elaborate outline catalogued in language that is relentlessly, aggressively—*annoyingly*—talky. One reads *American Pastoral* with the sense that Roth has compiled detailed notes on his characters' lives but never bothered to imagine the *story* those details should add up to; rather, he leaves this task to his readers, knowing, I suppose, that for him, for Philip Roth, for the author of *Goodbye, Columbus* and *Portnoy's Complaint* and *The Ghost Writer* and *The Counterlife* and the book that won last year's National Book Award, for a writer who has been since the begin-

ning of his career one of the most celebrated writers in America, they'll do it.

The phrase I am avoiding in this list of accolades is *resting
on his laurels*, and, although Roth's book, and, indeed, Roth's career, is full of problems, that is not one of them. In the conservative contemporary American literary landscape, Philip Roth
is the only one of our anointed writers still willing to reinvent
himself and his writing, to experiment with new forms in a
public venue and so risk failing before his large and rather
adoring audience, and for that alone he deserves admiration.
No, it's not laziness that mars *American Pastoral*, but a puzzling
lack of engagement with his story that makes for an arm's-
length, attenuated reading experience. The word I am avoiding
now is *boring*, but *American Pastoral* is such an odd, maddening
book that it is never quite boring; what it is, really, is a phantom
novel, a palimpsest, to borrow the term Gore Vidal used for his
recent memoirs. Vidal's palimpsest was merely a metaphorical
conceit, but it seems to me that Roth has created the genuine
article: a slather of words designed to mask the far more troubling story they cover.

Masks, of course, are Roth's stock in trade, and his most famous one, Nathan Zuckerman, the autobiographical stand-in
of several Roth novels as well as the commentator in Roth's
"autobiography," *The Facts*, is back in *American Pastoral*. In the
past Roth allowed Zuckerman to lag behind him a ways; now
he's pushed him on ahead. The new Zuckerman is old, impo-
tent, and incontinent; though he's survived the prostate cancer
that's killed many of his contemporaries, it is clearly a brief reprieve, and one suspects our next glimpse of Zuckerman will be
at his grave. The fear of death—or, if not fear, then at least the

confrontation of life's end—gives his story a tone that is ruminative, nostalgic, sometimes simply maudlin. This is hardly surprising, and I wouldn't even characterize it as detrimental—it's just something that comes with the territory—if that's not all the story was. But, alas, it is. *American Pastoral* is like watery oatmeal, the oats being Zuckerman's mishmashed reflections about the novel's declared subject, Seymour "the Swede" Levov, the water the never-fully-articulated reasoning why Zuckerman, and, by extension, Roth, has decided to write about him.

What it seems to boil down to is this: Roth/Zuckerman has always been fascinated by the spin that immigrant Jews have put on the quintessentially American experience of assimilation, largely, it seemed, because he viewed it as not just impossible but undesirable. Now, at the end of his life, he is reconsidering that position. Maybe assimilation, the desire to fit in—in what seems itself a gesture of assimilation, the not-quite-synonymous term Roth uses most often is "ordinariness"—is really all a man should hope for. To explore this option, Roth has created the ultimate assimilated Jew. Swede Levov is proudly, even triumphantly middle-class: he was a star athlete in high school, a marine right after college; he married Miss New Jersey and took over his father's glove factory; even his nickname reflects the fact that he *looks* like a goy, blond, blue-eyed, and gifted with a "steep-jawed, insentient Viking mask." The Swede is, in short, a hero, and, like most of his breed, a bit boring. In fact, he's a paper tiger, a sham of innocence and decency created solely so that he can be knocked down. Descriptions of his essential goodness bog down the novel at beginning and end, up to and including several pages in which the middle-aged Swede acts out a Johnny Appleseed fantasy so goofy that I'm still not convinced the intent wasn't parody. But the only way Roth can maintain the Swede's ordinariness is by allowing virtually nothing to happen in his life. I've already summarized most of *American Pastoral*'s "plot"— high school athlete, marine, husband, businessman—events, as I've said, which aren't seen by the reader, merely described by the author. The only thing I've left out is the bomb.

Ah, yes, the bomb.

The bomb is the novel's fulcrum, the single extraordinary event in a life that had been heretofore ordinary and that does everything it can to be ordinary afterward, a pivot so monumental that even after two hundred pages of explication and rumination it is little more than an offstage explosion, heard only as an echo, seen only in the bloodstained clothing on various characters as they emerge from the wings. The bomb is the device that Meredith "Merry" Levov, the Swede's only daughter, sets off in the Old Rimrock post office, ending one man's life and, more importantly, her father's happiness. The bomb has a Deep Meaning attached to it—it is 1968, and fourteen-year-old Merry has fallen in with a branch of the Weather Underground, and has set it off to protest the Vietnam War— but that explanation never rings true; like so much of the book, it is merely a cover-up. Merry sets off the bomb for the simple reason that she is fourteen and hates her parents, and she hates her parents because she stutters and cannot live up to the perfect example set by her all-star father and beauty queen mother.

Pages are devoted to the political arguments Merry has with her parents—conversations so divested of importance that they are decontextualized and merely listed as Conversation #1, #12, #18, and so on, all the way up to #67—but in the end each discussion is subsumed to the stutter, which her parents are spending a *fortune* on speech therapy to fix: "I'm not going to spend my whole life wrestling day and night with a fucking stutter when kids are b-b-b-being b-b-b-b-b-bu-bu-bu roasted alive by Lyndon B-b-b-baines b-b-b-bu-bu-burn-'em-up Johnson!" "What was the whole sick enterprise," is the Swede's ultimate assessment of the sixties, "other than angry, infantile egoism thinly disguised as identification with the oppressed?" As it happens, entire libraries have been filled with scholarship over the past three decades, attempting to determine just what "the whole sick enterprise" was, but Roth sticks to his line. After Merry bombs the post office, she goes into hiding, and, in a series of scenes that seem excerpted from a bad spy novel, the only contact the Swede has with her is through a go-between, Rita Cohen, "twenty-two years old, no more than five feet tall, and off on a reckless adventure with a very potent thing beyond her comprehension called power." The sentiment itself is trite, but the detail that rings false here is "no more than five feet tall." Why does it matter that Rita Cohen is short? Elsewhere Roth lashes out at her hippie hair and clothing—manufactured symbols of her countercultural beliefs—but why does her *size* disqualify her from "comprehending," let alone possessing power? In the same paragraph Roth refers to the Swede as a "conservatively dressed success story six feet three inches tall and worth millions," and it was, finally, the odd conjunction of these two details that enabled me to realize that, in Roth's view, economic and political power are extensions of physical power, and as such the logical possessions of the physically powerful, which—to cut to the chase—is a traditionally male province. Rita Cohen and Merry Levov ought not to have the power they do because they are not physically strong enough to wield it, and they are not physically strong enough to wield it because they are girls,

> so many were girls, girls whose political identity was total, who were no less aggressive and militant, no less drawn to "armed action" than the boys. There is something terrifyingly pure about their violence and the thirst for self-transformation. They renounce their roots to take as their models the revolutionaries whose conviction is enacted most ruthlessly. They manufacture like unstoppable machines the abhorrence that propels their steely idealism. Their rage is combustible. They are willing to do anything they can imagine to make history change. The draft isn't even hanging over their heads; they sign on freely and fearlessly to terrorize against the war, competent to rob at gunpoint, equipped in every way to maim and kill with explosives, undeterred by fear or doubt or inner contradiction—girls in hiding, dangerous girls, attackers, implacably extremist, completely unsociable.

Any writer charged with reviewing a Roth novel must decide if and when to raise the specter of the misogyny that has haunted so many of his books. Were Roth a writer of less talent, or less stature, the issue would be simpler; one could simply dis him and be done with it. But Roth has much of importance to say about contemporary Jews, in America, in England, in Israel, and about their relationship to the Gentile world; and, as well, his misogyny is often almost excusable—I stress *almost*—

merely the least effective answer to important questions he raises about the relationships between sons and mothers or husbands and wives. And it's not really the misogyny in this passage that takes the breath away as much as it is the *gynophobia*, the refusal to comprehend that women might have a stake in the most serious political questions of their time—"the draft isn't even hanging over their heads"—and so might want to do something to address those questions. It was when I read this passage, some 250 pages into *American Pastoral*'s muddled plot, that I realized, finally, that the true focus of Roth's novel had nothing to do with its declared narrative subject, namely, the "breakdown of the social fabric"[1] in America in the sixties, but of the threat posed by ungoverned female sexuality to all that is good (and male) in the world. The reason why *American Pastoral*'s plot seems only half there is because it *is*. The real narrative interest resides not in the text but in the subtext: how women, when they take power that is not rightfully theirs, betray and attack and destroy all they can.

Once this text is viewed as an elaborate narration of a misogynist fantasy, everything begins to fall in place. The heretofore inexplicable riff on Angela Davis—whose "hair reminds the Swede of Rita Cohen," the "extraordinary" hair, which "says, 'Do not approach if you don't like pain' "—is an illustration of dangerously unfettered female sexuality; whereas Vicki (no last name needed), black forelady of the Swede's glove factory, with her dutiful subservience to her boss—she "would not desert him. She told him, 'This is mine too. You just own

---

[1] Such a phrase could only come from a publisher's press release or jacket copy; in this case the culprit is the latter.

it' "—saves his factory from the Newark riots of July 1967. In
the Swede's last contact with Rita Cohen, she attempts to se-
duce him in a hotel room.

> She edged her two hands down onto her pubic hair. "Look at
> it," she told him and, by rolling the labia lips outward with
> her fingers, exposed to him the membranous tissue veined
> and mottled and waxy with the moist tulip sheen of flayed
> flesh. He looked away.
>
> "It's a jungle down there," she said. "Nothing in its
> place. Nothing on the left side like anything on the right
> side. How many extras are there? Nobody knows. Too many
> to count. There are glands down there. There's another
> hole. There are flaps. Don't you see what this has to do with
> what happened? Take a look. Take a good long look."

Seduction? Hardly. It's nothing more than a moral parable: the
vagina, jungle-like, is its own Vietnam, the perfect foible for
what Rita calls the Swede's "pillar of society." If Rita Cohen
represents one extreme of what happens to women who seize
power that isn't theirs—she becomes nothing but a consuming
hole—then the more fragile Merry represents the other: she is
consumed by the power she wields until she becomes less than
human. When, five years after the bombing, the Swede is re-
united with his daughter, it is only to discover that she has become a Jain, a member of a "relatively small Indian religious
sect" so committed to nonviolence that its members refuse to
wash lest they harm the microorganisms living on their bodies,
and whose most devout adherents eventually die of starvation
rather than kill plant life to eat. Merry is unwashed and fetid—
and, miraculously, cured of her stutter—but what the Swede

"saw sitting before him was not a daughter, a woman, or a girl; what he saw, in a scarecrow's clothes, stick-skinny as a scarecrow, was the scantiest farmyard emblem of life, a travestied mock-up of a human being, so meager a likeness to a Levov it could have fooled only a bird."

From here on out it's all denouement, an incredibly protracted, 150-page anticlimax that Roth has unironically entitled "Paradise Lost" (the middle chapter, devoted to the bomb, is called "The Fall," and the opening chapter, which establishes the Nathan Zuckerman conceit, is called "Paradise Remembered"). Roth's "Paradise Lost" takes place on the evening following the Swede's brief encounter with his daughter; the chapter is a set piece revolving around a dinner whose guests are the Swede and his wife; his parents, Sylvia and Lou; the Orcutts, his WASP neighbors (Bill's having an affair with the Swede's wife and Jessie's a drunk); the Umanoffs (Barry, the Swede's oldest friend, and his wife, Marcia, the "literature professor" who encouraged Merry in her early forays into radical politics); and the Salzmans, Shelly and Sheila, the latter being the Swede's former mistress and the person who harbored Merry after she set off the bomb. It's an amazingly social scene for a novel which has been claustrophobic until this point, never allowing more than three characters on any given page.

At dinner the conversation was about Watergate and about *Deep Throat.* . . . What surprised him, Shelly Salzman was saying, was that the electorate who overwhelmingly chose as president and vice president Republican politicians hypocritically pretending to deep moral piety should make a hit out of a movie that so graphically caricatured acts of oral sex.

What follows is an interplay of conservative politics and a discussion of how Linda Lovelace, the star of *Deep Throat*, is—well, I'll let Lou Levov, the novel's patriarch, explain it to you: "Adolf Hitler had the time of his life, Professor, shoveling Jews into the furnace. That does not make it *right*. This is a woman who is poisoning young minds, poisoning the country, and in the bargain she *is* making herself the scum of the earth—period!" For this, presumably, and for the kindness he shows to drunken Jessie Orcutt, Levov père is rewarded with a phallically thrust fork in the eye, delivered by Jessie Orcutt, and then Marcia Umanoff—the "Professor" referred to in Lou Levov's tirade against Hitler and Lovelace, an "unimpeded social critic in a caftan"—begins to "laugh and laugh and laugh at them all, pillars of a society that, much to her delight was going rapidly under." And there, abruptly, with neither bang nor whimper, the novel ends.

AND THEN OF COURSE there's the title. *American Pastoral:* as self-consciously literary and allusive a title as they come. But to what, exactly, does it allude? American literature began with the pastoral. In fact, our earliest literature wasn't particularly literary; it was primarily the work of diarists and letter writers recording their first experiences of the New World to secure more money from their benefactors, and these first diaries and letters record in unambiguous terms the rape of a virgin land. Time and again the New World was described as a woman, ei-

ther a voluptuous woman of many "fair endowments," including "goodly groves of trees, dainty fine round rising hillocks,
delicate fair large plains, sweet crystal fountains, and clear run-
ning streams that twine in fine meanders through the meads,
making so sweet a murmuring noise to hear as would even lull
the senses with delight asleep,"[2] or as a harsh mistress, against
whom "our extreme toil in bearing and planting palisades so
strained and bruised us and our continual labor in the extremity of the heat had so weakened us, as were cause sufficient to
have made us as miserable in our native country or any other
place in the world."[3] In either case, the land-woman had to be
subdued, and subdued it was, both physically by its colonists,
and figuratively, in the three and half centuries of literature
that have been produced here: think of Twain's *Huckleberry
Finn*, Dos Passos' *U.S.A.*, Nabokov's *Lolita*. In each of these
novels a feminized landscape is traversed, mapped, *contained*. In
our country, the pastoral is a false tradition, an invention, a
written convention, a way of writing about a subject originally
designed to woo money from investors who had no knowledge
of what was being written about; similarly, Roth's pastoral is
equally faked, a lost paradise that never existed but nevertheless had to be invented so it could be eulogized in his novel.
Roth's thesis, one that he's stated both in and out of his novels,
is that society changed irrevocably in the sixties—for this he
needs to write a book?—but, looked at from the long view, the
lay of the land appears to be pretty much unchanged.

---

[2] Thomas Morton, *New English Canaan*, c. 1630.
[3] John Smith, *The General History of Virginia*, 1624. The author is the same
John Smith made famous by his association with Pocahontas.

5

Digging for Gold

John Henry Days by Colson Whitehead

"Not since *Invisible Man...*" seems to be the critical commendation of choice for young black writers. In fact it's hard to imagine *any* book reproducing the tortured Dostoevskyian anxiety around race that energizes Ellison's historically important but wildly uneven novel, and, regardless of intention, the approbation almost always functions as doublespeak, proffering both canonical elevation and racial pigeonholing with the same benighting thumbprint. Its heavy impress can be found on the cover of *The Intuitionist*, Colson Whitehead's debut novel, where it seems particularly out of place. That book's clever elevator-inspection conceit served as a metaphor for all cultural hierarchies, political, scientific, philosophical, sexual, and, yes, racial. Whitehead neither shied away from nor privileged race over other concerns—particularly aesthetics—and if any relationship exists between *The Intuitionist* and *Invisible Man* it's a temporal one, a record of the exodus of racial anxieties from the authorial to the critical

sphere. Let Walter Kirn (or the editor who plucked this particular pull quote from Kirn's original review) limit his gaze to
"racial allegories": Colson Whitehead has his sights set on all
of America.

In fact Whitehead's ambitions are so vast they seem to
have snowed readers into confusing intended with actual product. *The Intuitionist* is a stiff, schematic novel whose most far-
reaching passages—the stuff about theoretical elevators, the
faux-noir torture bits—fall flattest; in particular, the novel's
protagonist, Lila Mae Watson, is weirdly emotionless, simultaneously three-dimensional but without substance, like a figure
half materialized on the transporter deck of the *Enterprise*.
You can see her, but you can't touch her, hear her, smell her, feel
her. J. Sutter, the protagonist of Whitehead's second novel,
John Henry Days, doesn't suffer from that problem. He's all
there—but he's also drowning in a swamp of extraneous material. Let's start there: *John Henry Days* is divided into two narrative streams, and it's the back story, a sort of free-association
pan-historical picking at the smorgasbord of the John Henry
fable, that is, initially, most compelling. Whitehead imagines
scenarios from the point of view of John Henry himself, as well
as a Depression-era black historian researching the possible
truth of the legend, a Jewish songwriter who copyrights the
ballad, a drunken blues singer who records an early version of
it, a Harlem businessman who builds a shrine to John Henry in
his apartment, and so on. Whitehead's point is simple, and fine:
cultural myths aren't made, but rather accrue their power
through a mixture of will and chance, artful addition and random accretion; they're one of the rare instances where the
blurred boundary between fiction and invention is actually in-

teresting, pricking as they do at the unscratchable itch to know where we come from.

True enough, but the problem here isn't the individual chapters; rather, it's the mass of them. Novels are infinite in scope, which is why one of the first things readers look for when they start a book is the author-imposed limits of the story at hand. It's these boundaries that give what they contain shape, beauty, meaning, in the same way that the formal constraints of a sonnet or a haiku simultaneously compress and amplify the words whose shape they dictate. But Whitehead's conceptual canvas is nearly as large as Borges' library of Babel, more than a century's worth of real and imagined characters whose association with John Henry—man, song, legend, ceramic statue, or postage stamp—is often tangential at best. It only takes one or two of these chapters to make Whitehead's point, after which they come to seem like digressions, and the vast middle of Whitehead's novel feels like the doughy center of a half-baked cake.

This back story doesn't really appear until page 83, but I started here because for all its flaws it's still the best part of the book, especially, as I said, if one considers the chapters individually rather than collectively. In particular, Whitehead's wildly erratic prose settles down when he imagines a history and characters removed from his own times. Compare, for example, these two passages:

> The first blow shattered half the bones in the boy's hand and the second blow shattered the other half. There was no way he could stop his hammer coming down the second time. . . . That night in the grading camp someone said they could

hear the boy's scream all the way on top of the mountain and down the shafts, louder than the sound of blasting. The boy's hand was all chewed up. The doctors would have to cut it off.

And:

They turn to see Tiny and Frenchie, two fellow mercenaries in their covert war against the literate of America. Hail, hail. They encounter each other on the newsstands, they chafe against one another in the contributors' notes of glossy magazines, but primarily they meet like this, on the eve of war, hungry, sniffing comps and gratis, these things like smoke from a freebie battlefield on the other side of morning. At stake: the primal American right of free speech, the freedom, without fear of censor, to beguile, confuse and otherwise distract the people into plodding obeisance of pop.

In the first passage the meaning arises naturally from what is described; in the second description is omitted in favor of exposition. Whitehead seems simultaneously to be looking for a point to his anecdote and desperate to ensure that the reader doesn't miss it, and the fact that the sentiment expressed is one which can be read "on the newsstands" and in "glossy magazines" doesn't help matters any. The result of this and many other bombastic passages is an objectification of the situations and characters it renders, in particular the aforementioned J. Sutter. J. is yet another "mercenary" whose existential crisis vis-à-vis the "pop" he purveys seems predicated upon the shattering of his youthful ideals during an internship at the *Down-*

town News (a satirized version of the *Village Voice*). By the time the novel opens J. has been making the rounds of the junket circuit for years—restaurant and club openings; record, magazine, and book launches; the occasional puff piece for a travel magazine—and as we join him he's en route to Talcott, West Virginia, the reputed location of John Henry's race against the steam shovel, and the site of the first annual John Henry Days, whose inaugural event coincides with the issuing of a commemorative John Henry stamp.

All of this is more context than narrative, an attempt to rest the novel's thin front story on the more substantial foundation of its back—a statuette, as it were, perched on an outsize concrete plinth. The actual story, such as it is, is revealed in a flash-forward on pages 24 to 26: on the last day of the John Henry festivities someone shoots three people before he's gunned down himself. This is the only flash-forward in the entire novel, and it betrays a well-founded mistrust of the book's ability to hold its readers' attention. Whitehead spends the following 363 pages playing catch-up, so that by the time we reach the end we know who went postal, just as we know that it was errant police bullets rather than the assassin's which killed two of the four journalists at the party and injured a third; what we never learn is whether J. was one of those shot, let alone killed, or if he was the one who got away.

Thematically, this would appear to be related to the fact that the existence of an actual John Henry remains unproven; thus the fate of J., our latter-day John Henry, must be similarly shrouded. And herein lies the logical flaw in Whitehead's bifurcated narrative. The mystery shrouding John Henry isn't a result of obfuscation but simply one of history's losses. The relevant pieces of paper disappeared, the knowing voices were, for whatever reason, silenced or never recorded; so it is with King Arthur, Atlantis, the Norsemen who landed on Greenland hundreds of years before Columbus. Instead of focusing on the one human relationship that develops in the novel, a near-romance between J. and a woman whose childhood was ruined by a father obsessed with John Henry memorabilia, Whitehead squanders his and our time on goofy commentary from disembodied postal workers and reports from philatelic newsletters, or on coyly circling the question of J.'s death or survival. The cryptic "there is still time" with which he closes the novel seems less a reprieve to J. than a final taunt at readers: still time to *what?*

Finally, it should be pointed out that John Sutter was the man on whose land gold was so famously discovered by James Marshall in California in 1848. What is perhaps less well-known is that neither Sutter nor Marshall profited from this discovery: hordes of prospectors swarmed Sutter's land, killing his cattle, destroying his crops, and plundering the riches they found; and both Sutter and Marshall died paupers. You can read about *that* in any encyclopedia, and if in fact Whitehead sees his protagonist as mine rather than mineral, that would make him his own Marshall, his readers the greedy prospectors. That's a nice point—you could even say there's a novel in it—but when the sand is sifted away the pan comes up empty.

6

In the Box

The Autobiography of My Mother by Jamaica Kincaid
How Stella Got Her Groove Back by Terry McMillan
Push by Sapphire

Every once in a while a reviewer is fortunate enough to find in his hands three or four or five books whose shared aesthetic and thematic concerns mark a distinct shift from those which have preceded them, and which afford the reviewer the singular privilege of announcing a new school of writing. It's an idea, an image really, which has attracted me ever since I read Edmund Wilson's early reviews of Stein, Hemingway, Woolf, and Joyce; here was a man who, in the course of meeting his weekly deadline, just happened to chart the birth of modernism. Oh sure, there was an element of luck involved—how often does a *Ulysses* just drop onto your desk?—but there was a certain skill on Wilson's part too, an eye keen enough to discern genius and a voice skilled enough to shill for the new literature without being shrill about it. Still, it's not exactly something a critic can *plan* for. Revolutions in the way literature is made occur maybe once or twice in a lifetime; and, as well, it takes such truly seismic shifts to spur the critical establishment to recognize the new movement. Modernism and postmodernism are the last two such radical restructurings of literary taste that I can think of, and the latter, depending on how you date it, is at least a half century old. It sort of begs the question, doesn't it? I mean, isn't it time for something new?

Well relax, folks. This isn't one of those times.

Still, I don't think I'm the only person who wishes it were. I think, in fact, that a lot of people are looking for something fresh in literature, and they've been looking, a little desperately if you ask me, for at least twenty-five years—since around the time Thomas Pynchon lobbed *Gravity's Rainbow* at an unsuspecting public. But it seems to me that the majority of those who are looking are doing so not at journals like the *London Review of Books* (or the *New Republic*, where Wilson was a columnist), or in the academy, but at the marketing meetings of major publishing houses, where bottom-line logic demands a new literary "movement" every five years or so—and, more importantly, a new market for that literature. It's this situation that seems to account for the fact that the nearer one comes to a contemporary point of view the more likely it is that a single thread of literature's tapestry will have been worried loose from the main and gifted—or saddled—with a name of its own. Think of the dirty realism of the early eighties, a term whose sole raison d'être seemed to be to place Raymond Carver in a marketable context; or the Brat Pack writers of the late eighties, whose three "founders," Jay McInerney, Bret Easton Ellis, and Tama Janowitz, remain its only viable practitioners; or the so-called New Narrativists of the first half of this decade, writers as diverse in talent and sensibility as Rebecca Brown, Dennis Cooper, Kathy Acker, Gary Indiana, and Sarah Schulman, writers whose primary similarity seemed to be that they all started out at small presses before being "discovered" by big houses.

By now—by which I mean, in the most Nixonian sense of the phrase, at this point in time—the formation and arrival of new schools of literature has become a given, a plot point in a narrative as familiar as a John Grisham thriller or a Danielle Steele romance: somewhere, "out there," a few writers are preparing the "next big thing," and these writers will "unexpectedly emerge," usually at a time when critics are bemoaning the lack of fresh talent on the literary scene. Three seems to be the generally accepted minimum number of writers needed to announce a new school, as in the McInerney-Ellis-Janowitz school, or the Kerouac-Burroughs-Ginsberg school, and I'm sure that more than a few sighs of relief were heard in the meeting rooms of New York publishing houses when the novels of Isabel Allende first began appearing in English, so that her name could be added to that of Gabriel García Márquez and, um, Jorge Luis Borges? and a decades-old phenomenon combining certain characteristically postmodern elements with certain characteristically gothic elements could be given the rejuvenating moniker "magic realism," and the career of Louise Erdrich was made.

None of this is, by the way, particularly bad. Silly: yes. Distracting: usually. Necessary: well, probably. Certainly from a marketing point of view, but from a critical standpoint there's something to be gained by charting the minutiae of stylistic and formal innovation. Henry James and James Joyce, for example, seem hardly to be writing in the same language, let alone the same century, but if one inserts a few writers between them—Edith Wharton, say, and Joseph Conrad, and Ernest Hemingway—then the journey from *The Portrait of a Lady* to *A Portrait of the Artist* seems not that long at all (I'm squishing the chronology a bit, but you see my point). Still, times have changed since the modernists pulled the well-worn carpet from beneath the feet of the Victorians. Back then, it seemed that the old guard yielded to the *avant* only when the former had exhausted its aesthetic possibilities and, as well, no longer reflected or commented on the changing world. Nowadays, however, the world is changing every five minutes or so, or so it would seem, given how often literature is said to change. But let's face it: the world may be changing but literature hasn't done much to keep up with it in a while. Modernism is for all intents and purposes dead, and postmodernism, while it has its die-hard adherents, seems at this point like a footnote that doesn't know when to stop. It is, in fact, Victorian realism, one foot firmly planted in the domestic observation of Flaubert and the other in the social satire of Dickens, that holds center stage today; indeed, after modernism first ran its course the realists returned to the fore; then, for a while, there was postmodernism, but that too retreated and realism returned; now, what one hears hailed as an emerging new genre of writing usually turns out to be nothing more than a standard realist text inflected by a preoccupation with some subject or other. The dirty realists liked to write about trailer homes and motels, the Brat Packers liked nightclubs and drug addicts, the New Narrativists were partial to sexual transgression and anticapitalist pronouncements. But whatever the sentiment, it was almost always couched in familiar realist terms, with perhaps an occasional pomo trick thrown in for effect.

And then, at some point, all of this devolved even further. What had formerly been a narrow-minded focus on subject matter became a rather more voyeuristic focus on author "identity"—that nineties buzzword for the sociocultural and ethnic background of a writer, duly registered in the photo and bio that appear on the inside back flap of new hardcovers. For example, writing with gay content, which in terms of number of books published had been thriving since the early seventies, didn't become the phenomenon Gay Writing until articles in *Publishers Weekly* and the *New York Times* declared it one of the fastest growing niche markets in publishing. I cite this particular example because it seems to me that the official recognition of gay writing crystallized a trend not merely to subjugate aesthetic issues in favor of certain assumptions based on a writer's identity, but to suggest that the former actually *follow* from the latter. This is, of course, simplistic, if not simply spurious: *The Age of Innocence* and *Moby-Dick*, two books by white authors, are both populated by white characters, but knowing that doesn't give you any indication, in the first place, of what the books are *about*, and, in the second, it doesn't mean that the books exist in any but the most obvious of relationships to each other (the relationship in this case being that they both happen to be sitting on my desk). Nevertheless, and especially in the case of writers who are not white—or not straight, or not male—such crudely drawn sociological lines have become de rigueur, a crudity propagated not just by the conservative impulse of marketing meetings, but by the supposedly radical impulse of identity politicking. I don't mean to characterize it as a no-win situation—it's certainly been successful in moving a lot of worthwhile books that ten or fifteen years ago would never have been published—but I do think it's skewed the way in which these books are *read*. To put it simply, the combination of politicized contextualizing ("Black Is Beautiful," "Gay Is Good") and marketing hype ("Buy Black," "Get Gay") have conspired to convince readers that a lot of recherché books are fresh, exciting, and distinct from what has gone before, despite the fact that such divisions have about as much validity as the chalk line Lucy used to draw down the center of the apartment she shared with Ricky, splitting couch, table, and coffee pot in half.

All of this by way of introduction to the books under review here. Their three authors are all black; they are also all women, and they are also—or almost—all American (Jamaica Kincaid was born in Antigua, but she left there at seventeen and has lived in the United States for the past thirty years), and it is primarily for these reasons that they are being reviewed together. I say primarily, because there is the added factor that writing by black women in America is probably the most successful in both critical and commercial terms of all the identity-defined categories of writing around. When I was first asked to review these books together, I admit I was both curious and a bit put off: I wondered if this random gathering could, in fact, add up to some kind of coherent portrait about the condition of black women in America today, whether that portrait was rendered in aesthetic terms or sociological ones; or if, as I suspected, that here were three texts which had little to say about the real world and even less to say to one another. I use the word *texts* here, as opposed to the word *writers* because, while I'm sure Jamaica Kincaid, Terry McMillan, and Sapphire could have a perfectly nice conversation, I'm equally sure that their books, if given their druthers, wouldn't be caught dead on the same shelf.

Depending on your point of view, the phenomenon of black women's writing could be said to have begun all the way back in the Harlem Renaissance. Though the men of the period are better known, the thirties and forties also produced noteworthy work by Dorothy West, Ann Petry, and Gwendolyn Brooks among others, as well as the great Zora Neale Hurston. Others might date it to the late sixties and early seventies, when such writers as Nikki Giovanni, Toni Cade Bambara, Ntozake Shange, Sonia Sanchez, and Paule Marshall helped redefine and expand the parameters of the mainstream in American publishing. This "middle period" was, I think, capped in 1982 by the publication of Alice Walker's Pulitzer Prize–winning *The Color Purple.* In that novel, Celie, the protagonist, teaches herself to read and write, and what she writes down is her own story; in doing so, she symbolically reenacts what a generation of black women readers and writers had just done themselves. But I don't think that black women's writing could really be called a "phenomenon" until 1992, when Terry McMillan's *Waiting to Exhale* came more or less out of nowhere to become a runaway bestseller and one of the most talked about novels of that year; 1992 also saw bestsellers by Toni Morrison (*Jazz*) and Alice Walker (*Possessing the Secret of Joy*); the following year Maya Angelou created a sensation by declaiming (*On the Pulse of Morning*) at Bill Clinton's first inauguration, Rita Dove was appointed U.S. Poet Laureate, and, the icing on the cake, Toni

Morrison was awarded the Nobel Prize. A year after publishing *The Color Purple*, Alice Walker wrote, "I write all the things *I should have been able to read*"; ten years later, not only was she reading them, but so was much of America.

Such a transformation—from a situation in which the presence of a few celebrated writers only heightened the general absence of black women from American letters, to a situation in which new black women writers like Veronica Chambers, Edwidge Danticat, and A.J. Verdelle appear every month—raises all sorts of questions. The most important one, of course, is *how did it happen*, the answer to which would require a discussion of the tendency of the post–World War II critical establishment to laud books with a "positive social message" over those which seemed "socially disengaged" and "aesthetically decadent"; not to mention fairly complete histories of the civil rights *and* feminist movements. But on a more basic, and base, level it has a lot to do with the fact that the publishing industry seems finally to have realized that twenty-two million African Americans are *not* a negligible consumer group, and that, as well, if white Americans could be convinced to buy books by blacks—as the recording industry had done so well with jazz, blues, rock, and rap—then a *lot* of books could be sold. If the books happened to earn their writer a Pulitzer or a Nobel Prize, that was great— but if they could move a million copies in hardback and generate a hit movie, so much the better. Which brings us, finally, to the subject at hand: three books by three black women which either sold quite well, or were expected to (the speculation in New York as to how much Sapphire was actually paid for the hundred-page manuscript of *Push*—the figure I heard most often was half a million dollars—has only recently been

eclipsed by the speculation as to how much its publisher is los-
ing on the deal).

Let's start at the bottom. Terry McMillan's *How Stella
Got Her Groove Back* is the most lazily written book I've
ever read. Some people—namely, the book's publishers—
might be inclined to characterize its style as "breathless," but
I think of it as a panting, gasping, protracted death rattle:
four hundred pages of unpunctuated run-on sentences about
virtually nothing. It is, in fact, very hard to believe that any
part of *Stella* was actually *written*. I imagine McMillan dic-
tating it into a microcassette recorder while doing her daily
two miles on her personal treadmill (hence the breathless
comment). *Stella*'s plot: a forty-something black business-
woman on vacation in Jamaica is smitten with a twenty-year-
old stud who immediately falls for her, leaving Stella with
nothing to do but kvetch for what feels like a contractually obligated number of pages before she predictably gives in and
everyone lives H.E.A. (happily ever after). Stella's kvetching is
punctuated by only two diversions: her tendency to constantly
worry if one or another of her bodily orifices is emitting a foul
smell (McMillan's heroine chooses the food she eats based on
its ability to clean her palate, and she obsesses about douching
in a manner reminiscent of Lady Macbeth's preoccupation with
her hands); and her insistent plugging of consumer products
made by or of significance to black people. Oprah is the recipient of McMillan's largesse (as McMillan has been the recipient
of Oprah's), and Montell Jordan, and Seal, and MTV in general, not to mention the Toyota Land Cruiser and anything
with a BMW emblem on it, but McMillan saves up an entire
page for herself:

I decide to sit out on my balcony and read a little of *The Grace of Great Things* by Robert Grudin which sounded good when I read the book jacket in the store but it turns out to be too academic and deep and not exactly beach reading so I put it down after a half hour and pick up *Black Betty* by Walter Mosley which I've been meaning to read since I read and loved *Devil in a Blue Dress* but there's already a grisly murder on page two of *Black Betty* and I'm not much in the mood for death. I pick up the hardcover version [natch] of *Waiting to Exhale* by that Terry McMillan which I bought when it first came out and I've been meaning to read for a couple of years now and after reading like the first fifty or sixty pages I don't know what all the hoopla is about and why everybody thinks she's such a hot writer because her shit is kind of weak when you get right down to it and this book here has absolutely no literary merit whatsoever at least none that I can see and she uses entirely too much profanity. Hell I could write the same stuff she writes. . . .

McMillan goes on about herself, but I have only one thing left to say. Nearly every person I talked to about McMillan excused her egregious lack of talent by referring to her as a sort of black Danielle Steele—although no one would say so in print, lest it be considered insulting to McMillan. In fact, the comment only insults Steele, a professional who delivers at least one new book to her fans a year, each of which features a detailed and properly formulaic plot told through simple, grammatically correct sentences. Steele doesn't waste her readers' time with solipsistic references to her own books—that's what an author bio is for—or load them down with detailed shopping lists in an effort to invest her work with sociocultural significance. I was going to say that McMillan could profit by reading a few of Steele's books, but profit is the one thing McMillan *is* good at making; I'm not sure what, if anything, could help the books.

The only advantage Sapphire's *Push* has over McMillan's *Stella* is that it's short. There are only 142 tiny pages of what you'd call "text," followed by an additional twenty pages or so—the pages are unnumbered to emphasize their extraneous nature—of poems and journal entries by the fictitious members of a teen literacy program. The literacy program is where readers last see the novel's protagonist, Precious Jones. Before she gets there Precious must first bear two children by her father, one of which has Down Syndrome and is named Little Mongo. It was at that point that I started giggling, and I tittered all the way through Precious' subsequent trials, each of which is so crudely drawn that the comedy I saw in them seemed intentional—there is little to distinguish this narrative from a David Sedaris story, save that Sedaris shows more restraint. After her rapist father abandons the family to the perils of the welfare state, Precious is first physically and then sexually assaulted by her mother, a woman so overweight that she can't leave her own apartment; Precious' mother also forces Precious to eat fattening food, seemingly in an effort to make her daughter as big as she is. Little Mongo and baby Abdul are taken from Precious by the state; Precious is kicked out of school for behavior problems and because she can't read (it's not her fault, she's got troubles, and besides, she's dyslexic too); then, finally, she learns she's HIV-positive. Still, these tragedies are somehow contextualized—or, in classic liberal patois, ameliorated—by the fact that Precious is taught to read by a les-

bian named Blue Rain. All told, Sapphire has written a slim
piece of propaganda designed to deliver the novel message that
father-daughter rape is a bad thing and literacy a good thing,
with white people falling somewhere in between, and if you
thought of *The Color Purple* before reading the second half of
this sentence then you're way ahead of Sapphire's game. But
unlike Alice Walker's novel—or, for that matter, Toni Morrison's *The Bluest Eye—Push* has all the grace and subtlety of a
television drama of the week: "Ms Rain say it's a big country.
Say bombs cost more than welfare. Bombs to murder kids 'n
shit. Guns to war people—all that cost more than milk 'n Pam-
pers. Say no shame. No shame."

What supposedly distinguishes *Push* from the sentimentality of any other issue-of-the-week moral tale is the "powerful,
uncompromising voice" (I am quoting from *Push*'s press release) in which it is written. As it happens, I missed both the
power and the lack of compromise; what I did notice was a lot
of profanity, which I often found very funny (although, again,
I'm not sure it was meant to be), and a *lot* of grammatical errors. Precious, as I said, is illiterate for much of the book's time-
line, and the grammatical errors and phonetic misspellings are
meant, I assume, to reflect this, just as the improved grammar
of the book's later sections reflects Precious' newfound mas-
tery of language; the whole enterprise is rendered nonsensical,
however, since we learn on the first page that the book's action
is told in flashback. Precious, in other words, has already
learned to write, and readers can only assume that she is affect-
ing her former illiteracy (Sapphire's intent is muddied still further by a seemingly random sixteen-page shift into third
person early in the book). As a gimmick, then, Sapphire's

grammatical butchery is both inconsistent and distracting; but the problem is more than aesthetic: in a book which supposedly gains its significance by its use of urban black English, Sapphire never distinguishes between the individual phenomenon of one character's inarticulateness and the cultural phenomenon of the disjunction between black and white English. In other words, *Push* implies that black English is nothing more than an inability of one segment of the population to speak properly. I don't think that's Sapphire's intention, you understand, but it's what comes across. It's a problem common to most propaganda: it can be turned against you almost as easily as it is deployed.

Of the three novels under review here, only Jamaica Kincaid's possesses anything like literary complexity—and that only if you've not read her earlier work. If you have, then you immediately recognize *The Autobiography of My Mother* as the latest and least effective iteration of the themes of her four earlier books, three works of fiction and a book-length essay, *A Small Place*, all of which use some rather lovely sentences to chronicle the condition of postcolonial life in the West Indies. The problem is that as time goes by Kincaid's sentences have gotten prettier and prettier—Wallace Stevens' "floribund," a term made from the combination of "florid" and "moribund," is what comes to mind—while her themes have been reduced to a few ideologically overdetermined situations. *Autobiography* probably deserves a longer, more focused reading than I give it here, but, just as the work of Terry McMillan and Sapphire has been bathed in the glow of real talents like Toni Morrison and Alice Walker, Kincaid's novel is dragged down by having to rub shoulders with dreck like *Stella* and *Push*. On its own I might merely have called the novel flawed, but, after wading through the first two novels to get to it, it was such an unsatisfactory destination that I can only call it bad.

The Autobiography of My Mother tells the life story of a post-colonial Caribbean woman whose mother dies, as the book's first sentence tells us, "at the moment I was born." The title, of course, is an oxymoron—one doesn't write someone else's autobiography—and it isn't explained until the novel's final pages, by which point the reader has learned almost nothing about the mother but has been saturated with the petty details of the novel's rather mean-spirited narrator (distant father, mean stepmother, tough life, loveless marriage, etc.). Then:

> This account of my life has been an account of my mother's life as much as it has been an account of mine, and even so, again it is an account of the life of the children I did not have, as it is their account of me. In me is the voice I never heard, the face I never saw, the being I came from. In me are the voices that should have come out of me, the faces I never allowed to form, the eyes I never allowed to see me. This account is an account of the person who was never allowed to be and an account of the person I did not allow myself to become.

Here is Kincaid's ear at its best and her mind at its worst. The prose is lovely, rhythmic, almost inexorable—and, I would argue, distinctly, beautifully American—yet the sentiments expressed by the words themselves are trite, falsely universalizing, and often just muddled. To be told at the end of a novel that one person is the same as that of any other seems to me not just dumb, but an insult to a reader's goodwill and perseverance.

But one is inclined to believe that Kincaid means what she writes, because this narrator is, in fact, virtually indistinguishable in psyche from the protagonists of *Lucy* or *Annie John*. Maybe Kincaid *does* think all Caribbean women lead the same life, but I suspect that Grace Jones might disagree with her.

Still, it's a charge that could be leveled against many, many authors, and it isn't in and of itself a weakness. A carpenter, for example, can be obsessed with pine, but he needn't build the same table over and over: he can build a chair, a bed, an entire house. But Kincaid has built the same box time and again, and with this statement she seems to have nailed herself inside. All that's left now is the burying—and not just, I hope, of Kincaid's need to render her characters' psyches indistinguishable just because they share a few commonalities of biography, but of the more odious real-world tendency to make the same sorts of reductive conclusions based on the artificial distinctions of identity-based categorization and its attendant focus-group literature. In point of fact the only thing "new" about black women's writing—or black male writing, or gay writing, or Jewish writing, or, what seems to be the newest fad, Latina writing—is the number of people who are buying it, and sales, I don't think, are quite what the term "movement" is meant to imply. The last twenty-five years have seen far too much speculation about one supposed literary movement after another, from leftist (and rightist) agitprop organizations to capitalist-minded publishers to critics eager to make a name for themselves. Still, it's hard to blame them, when the one group of people who *don't* seem to be interested in finding a new literature, or creating one, is writers.

7

The Tinkerbell Trick

Love, Etc. by Julian Barnes

Julian Barnes is a phrasemaker. He *loves* phrases. "Trust leads to betrayal." "The old are very good at being old, it is a skill they learn." "The rule about married sex . . . is that after a few years you aren't allowed to do anything you haven't done before." "Stuart, if you'll pardon the phrase, couldn't get any if he paid for it." "Do you know the phrase 'Information wants to be free'?" "The law of unintended effect. . . . Isn't that just a phrase written in neon? Put it up there alongside 'the word made flesh,' 'que sera, sera,' 'si monumentum requiris, circumspice,' 'horseman, pass by,' 'we have left undone those things which we ought to have done,' and 'with trembling hands, he undid her bra.' The law of unintended effect. Does that not explain your life even as it does mine?"

Not that there's anything wrong with phrases. "It is a truth universally acknowledged, that a single man in possession of a good fortune, must be in want of a wife." "All unhappy families are like one another; each unhappy family is unhappy in its own

way." "Our nada who art in nada, nada be thy name." But anyone who reads more than fifty pages of Julian Barnes can
see that his phrasemaking exacerbates the fundamental problem of his writing, which is that it's clever, tepid, and, finally,
soulless. In fact, soullessness in fiction is hard to come by (most
bad writing actually suffers from too much soul). A good
writer—Hemingway, Jean Rhys, Jim Thompson—works it to
horrifying effect by systematically stripping his or her characters of every attribute we think of as human, but it's the rare
writer, a writer like Julian Barnes, who seems not to recognize
the existence of those attributes in the first place, and as a result his characters smile and make the coffee and put a pretty
flip in their hair, and it's not until the smoke starts coming out
of their ears that we realize they're Stepford Wives. "We are all,
are we not, lost. Those who know it not are the more lost.
Those who do know it are found, for they have grasped their
full lostness." "Are we not . . . know it not . . . their full lostness." This is relatively harmless drivel, but it doesn't explain
why Barnes' writing crawls under your skin and itches like
scabies.

Take Barnes' 1991 novel *Talking It Over*. In that book Stuart was best friends with Oliver and married to Gillian until
Oliver seduced her, at which point Gillian divorced Stuart and
married Oliver and, well, you know the rest of the story. But in
case you don't there's *Love, Etc.*, which, despite its jacket copy
assertion that it bears an "eerie, freestanding relationship" to
Talking It Over, is in fact what is more commonly called a sequel. After a nine-year American sojourn, Stuart has reentered
Oliver and Gillian's down-at-the-heels existence and com-
menced a seduction of his own. The outcome of Stuart's ro-

mancing, however, is less clear than Oliver's, by which I mean that in the final pages of *Talking Redux* Gillian is pregnant with Stuart's baby, but whether she returns to Stuart, sticks with Oliver, or ditches both men is left unsaid. Barnes seems to have decided this time around to prep us for the sequel's sequel in the current cinematic manner, which is to say that he's put off the end of this book until, presumably, the beginning of the next.

Of course there's more to the story than that, but before you can get to it you must first get through the storytelling; I think, in fact, it's fair to claim that both *Talking It Over* and *Love, Etc.* are more concerned with telling than tale. In both novels, Barnes' lost characters directly address a "you" who might be a therapist or detective or some other interrogator, but soon enough turns out to be the reader him- or herself. Barnes has more fun with this device the first time out. Sometimes characters defend one another without seeming to realize they're being attacked behind their backs (dramatic irony, à la *Oedipus Rex*), other times they dispute one another's versions of events as if they're seated around the same conference table (unreliable narration, cf. *Rashomon*), and still other times they reach out to readers directly, reminding us that our faith in them is a condition for their continued existence (late Pirandello, or, for that matter, early Disney). The net effect of these asides is a mocking but not irreverent deconstruction of the traditional alliance between character and reader. Barnes scales the fourth wall but doesn't see fit to jump into the no-man's-land beyond it, and perhaps the most compelling aspect of his narrational device is the fact that the majority of his extratextual exchanges call to mind the fleshier relationship of audience to stage or screen. It's almost as if his characters were willing *us* to exist, rather than the other way around. I.e., Oliver: "Hi, I'm Oliver. Oliver Russell. Cigarette? No, I didn't think you would. Yes, I *do* know it's bad for my health." Or, later, Stuart: "Hello! We've met before. Stuart. Stuart Hughes. Yes, I *am* sure. Positive. About ten years ago."

Whether you go in for this kind of nontraditional narration (substitute "pomo shenanigans" or "postmodern experimentation" as you will) is a matter of taste. I've always been interested in it myself, and Barnes is, as I've said, a clever craftsman—clever enough to have come up with the device, and clever enough not to push it too far. And let's give him his due: for all his failings as a novelist, Julian Barnes is still smart enough to realize that contemporary writers haven't come close to exhausting the possibilities offered by the radical assault on the novel that characterized the fiction of the first sixty or seventy years of the last century. And unlike Joyce's bombast or Hemingway's inscrutability, Barnes' own investigations are consistently humorous, reader-friendly, *engaging*, which is perhaps why his writing has been significantly more popular during his lifetime than most modernist or postmodernist figures. Still, I can't help but wonder if it's that very lack of urgency which is the root cause of Barnes' soullessness. Literary modernism was a response to, among other things, the devastation of World War I and Victorian realism's failure to stave off, predict, or even quantify that conflagration; similarly, postmodernism was a reaction to the modernist failure vis-à-vis World War II. You can argue about the efficacy or appropriateness of such concerns all you want, but what's incontrovertible is that every so-called "experimental" writer from

Stein to Pynchon felt that his or her work addressed something of historical consequence. They considered their endeavors philosophical rather than merely aesthetic, whereas Julian Barnes, whose musings bear a surface resemblance to certain postmodern conventions, seems motivated by nothing more than boredom, decadence, or hubris.

Look what I can do! these novels boast at nearly every page. But the truth is Barnes' direct addresses to the reader do little more than nudge us in the ribs, and as one gets deeper into *Talking It Over* and *Love, Etc.* the limits of his narrative strategy become apparent. I once heard the novel defined as "everything not mentioned in the jacket copy," and by that yardstick there's not much book here at all. If anything there's less inside the covers than on them, where it's promised that Gillian will "veer[. . .]wildly" between Stuart and Oliver for a while. In fact she falls like a finger-flicked domino; it just takes her a couple hundred pages to hit the ground. To pad this nearly nonexistent narrative, Barnes allows ex-husbands and -wives to pop out of the woodwork and put in their two cents. Soon French mothers-in-law are spouting typically Gallic sentiments and American prostitutes' hooker-with-a-heart-of-gold wisdom comes to seem as relevant as anything anyone else has to say, but all these interruptions and asides do is remind us that the triumvirate of characters who are the ostensible subject of so much brouhaha are even flatter than the narrative they inhabit. It was Forster—the most understated and underrated of modernist figures—who famously said that a good novel is composed of round and flat characters. He allowed an exception in Dickens' work, whose characters, though flat, "vibrated wildly." But Julian Barnes' protagonists don't even do that. They merely acquire surface area as the rolling pin of his platen spreads them thinner and thinner.

To wit: "Oh shit," Oliver says without preamble in *Talking It Over*. "I'm in love with Gillie. . . . What's going to happen now?" One hundred forty-five pages later Gillie gives us the answer: "I loved Stuart. Now I love Oliver." In between these two plot points is what appears to be the traditional scenic connective tissue, but even though it clearly delineates the route from there to here—from Stuart's house, as it were, to Oliver's—it omits, like a road map, the mountain ranges, out-of-date billboards, and fleeting eye contact with the blonde in the Lexus that distinguish an actual journey from a line on a piece of paper: the traffic jams, the overpriced gas, the toll booths and speeding tickets, the rickety crosses with faded flowers commemorating a highway fatality, the good and bad weather, the good and bad coffee. What Barnes gives us is the obligatory scene of Oliver combing Gillian's hair while she works ("He does it every time now. My hair doesn't even have to be loose, he just takes the comb and undoes the clip and pulls the hair back and smoothes it down and puts the grip back in. And I'm burning."), but what his impressive string of conjunctions omits is the part where Gillian tells us why in the *hell* she decided to let Oliver into her studio in the first place, when he's all but propositioned her under her husband's nose. Though the hair-combing scene could work in any number of romantic buildups, it seems as out of place here as a tea party on the lip of a volcano; similarly, for all Barnes' mechanical delineation of Oliver's seduction ("and . . . and . . . and . . . and. . . . And . . ."), the key question of attraction is never addressed, and in the end the only discernible reason Gillian invites Oliver in is because Barnes programmed her to do it.

What's missing, in other words, is the epiphany. But as with the therapy sessions and talk shows Barnes' narrative method resembles, experience—the events that in a fictional context become plot—is presented retroactively. The suspense of discovery is gone, and the realizations that accompanied them have by now faded into something Barnes or his characters would like to pass off as wisdom. As Gillian says at the beginning of *Love, Etc.*, "What people want to know, whether they ask it directly or not, is how I fell in love with Stuart and married him, then fell in love with Oliver and married him, all within as short a space as is legally possible. Well, the answer is I did just that." The problem here isn't that Gillian's wrong, or that she's oversimplifying, but that she's right: her psyche is no more or less interesting than her schematic rendering of it, and as a result *Talking It Over* and *Love, Etc.* tend to read like précis ("I'm in love with Gillie, . . . What's going to happen now?") or summation ("I loved Stuart. Now I love Oliver.") and after a while it starts to feel like an Anglicized *Oprah* episode aimed at the aspiring bourgeoisie. And like the typical *Oprah* episode, these novels never get around to answering the hard questions. For example, why *would* Oliver attempt to steal the wife of his self-described "oldest friend"? And why is it that Stuart's oldest—read: only—friend is a man who does nothing but belittle him? And why, finally, does Gillian think Oliver would make a good husband and father, when he was dismissed from his most recent job as a high school teacher for attempting to force himself on one (or two, or more) of his students?

Of all the questions that Barnes avoids answering (or, for that matter, asking), this last is most important, because it's the only one that has any moral weight to it. You can tell it troubles Barnes as well, because he spends a lot of time attempting to play it down: though Oliver's boss "simperingly permitted the murky phrase *sexual harassment* to hover in the air between us," Oliver dismisses the affair as a mere *"contretemps,"* a "misunderstanding"; Stuart's catchphrase for what happened is "the old, old, sordid story," each of his "old"s making it that much less "sordid," whereas Gillian's equally evasive term is "molest." The word that all these euphemisms are avoiding is "rape," attempted, statutory, or otherwise, for the simple reason that it's a word of more consequence than Barnes' airy narrative can sustain. Nevertheless, the repressed sexual guilt surrounding Oliver's crimes becomes conflated with the characters' existential self-doubt ("if you decline to perceive me, then I really *shall* cease to exist"), until they finally surface in a narrative climax which, in plot terms, bears the same relationship to what's gone before as a terrorist attack does to a transatlantic flight: it's unexpected, destructive, and leaves behind little more than body parts floating in the water. What I mean is, the only time Barnes gets beyond his jacket copy is when he drops a bomb on everything he's built thus far.

But wait a moment, one can almost hear Barnes' supporters protesting. Don't give away the end just yet. Isn't it the defense of postmodern fiction that the traditional satisfactions of narrative storytelling are not its aim? The empathic connection between reader and character, these supporters will remind you—what's called identification in literature and transference in analysis—is willed by the former and not the latter, and (let's let them see their argument through to its conclusion) doesn't knowing how this equation works free the contemporary writer from the Victorian drudgery of making characters seem "real"?

The short answer to all this is, of course, yes, but that deferral to readerly assumptions comes with a price. Let me try to explain with an example. The single most important literary convention of the twentieth century was the double-spaced paragraph break. That gap could stand for anything: sex, sleep, a tedious taxi journey between apartment and opera house. It was the reason why, on the one hand, twentieth-century literary fiction was so much shorter than what preceded it—a double-spaced break could elide the passage of hours or years without troubling the reader, who filled in the gap with personal experience—but, on the other hand, it was also why most so-called departures from realism tended to reinforce the very suppositions that made realism possible in the first place. Call it postmodernism, call it shorthand, call it gloss: as the century progressed that reader-filled gap became simultaneously smaller and smaller and more and more common (like everything else, it became virtual), until it seemed that there was more conceptual air than text in virtually every major work written in the eighties. Think Ray Carver, Lorrie Moore, the Brat Pack—and how awful does most of that shit seem now?

To some degree, the big fat novels of the nineties are a reaction against this, a return to the written transition as it were, a reminder that in life there are no double-spaced breaks or fades to black: life doesn't happen in moments of being, it happens in moments of boredom. But the real master of this brand of pop postmodernism, Julian Barnes himself, has taken no notice. His novels get thinner and thinner even as his pronouncements within them grow more and more grand. Indeed, Barnes is such a virtuoso of the glib elision that it's almost possible to ignore the fact that what seems like writerly laziness is actually imaginative conservatism. Rather than question or trouble age-old notions about how people behave and how the world works, Barnes trades on them—indeed, depends on readers to use their conventional wisdom to bolster his aphoristic texts and fill in all the gaps his scattershot storytelling has left behind. And even this would be bearable if he would only follow his own rules. But he doesn't. Early in *Talking It Over*, Oliver declares, "I don't ever want to get old. Spare me that. Have you the power? No, even you don't have the power, alas." What Oliver is reminding us—and what his creator would do well to remember—is that the semblance of life readers give fictional characters inevitably follows the same rules their own lives obey. This is not to say that every character in every book will be born, grow old, and eventually die, but that, rather, every character in every book will be subject to the laws of whatever universe the writer has created for him or her, and, as such, if that universe bears more than a passing resemblance to the reader's universe, then yes, its inhabitants will be born, grow old, and die. And when that universe bears more than a passing resemblance to a universe in which it would be improbable that two men who loathe each other would refer to each other as best friends and well-nigh impossible that an educated woman would fall in love with a man who rapes teenaged girls, then there are bound to be some consequences when those contradictions are, in fact, untroubledly glossed over as nothing more than "the old, old, sordid story."

Those consequences finally manifest themselves in the brutal climaxes of both *Talking It Over* and *Love, Etc.* (yes, I *am* giving away the end, so stop reading now if you're still inclined to pick up one of these books). In *Talking It Over,* Barnes' comedy of manners about the most classic of love triangles is suddenly resolved by a scene that could have been lifted from *Blue Velvet.* Gillian, now married to Oliver, is worried that Stuart hasn't gotten over her (perhaps because he's followed his ex-wife and her new husband to a French village and is spying on them through the curtains of his hotel). In order to "free" Stuart from his love for her, Gillian manipulates Oliver into beating her while Stuart looks on. As she retells the story in *Love, Etc.:*

> I'd been getting at Oliver for a day or more, nagging at him, working him up to a pitch. It was all planned. All my plan. I knew Stuart would be watching. I made a very specific calculation. I thought that if Stuart could see Oliver being vile to me, and me being vile to Oliver, he'd think our marriage wasn't to be envied and that would help him get on with his own life. . . . I was standing there like a scarecrow, like a madwoman. The blood was from Oliver hitting me with the car keys in his hands. I knew the village's eyes were on me. . . . But of course the eyes which were on me that really counted were Stuart's. I knew he was there, up in his hotel room. And I was thinking: have I got away with it? Will I make it work?

As a friend of mine says, That is just so *wrong.* Its Lucille Ball logic would be laughable if it weren't coming out of Joan of Arc's mouth. The misogyny is so twisted it's hard to sort out where it begins and ends. A contemporary woman who actually thinks her husband will—and should—beat her after a day's bad behavior? Who thinks, further, that this will free her spurned lover from his affections? Who thinks, finally, that she's somehow obligated to do this because she switched affections midstream? If I didn't know better, I'd've guessed that Julian Barnes was born in eighteenth-century Salem rather than twentieth-century Leicester; and given the amount of space the opening pages of *Love, Etc.* devote to *Talking It Over*'s shocking finale, I'd've also thought some kind of redress was chief on Barnes' list in his sequel. But no. In *Love, Etc.*, stolid Stu returns, still in love with Gillian and ready to get rid of the Lancelottish Oliver once and for all. For two hundred dull pointless pages Stuart's selfless ministrations to his former wife seem to be wooing Gillian back to his camp when suddenly—to speed things along?—he rapes her in her living room while Oliver sleeps upstairs. The believability of the scene is further strained by the fact that Gillian never calls out for help and even covers up what happened at first, saying that she and Stuart had sex "like two hot kids in a kitchen, half-dressed, whispering, urgent" and then, ten pages later, reverses herself with the excuse "I wanted you to keep the good opinion you have of Stuart." In fact the only meaning that attaches to the scene is the ancient association of power with prowess: Stuart knocks down Gillian and knocks her up in the process, and if any doubt remained as to Gillian's manqué status, it's completely eradicated by her "I don't believe in abortion" speech, followed by her final question, which all but closes the novel:

> Does Stuart love me? Still? Really? As he said?
> > That's the key question.
> > What do you think?

Well, since you asked:

In lieu of the traditional satisfactions of fictional narrative—believable characters, satisfactory storylines, epiphanies and the like—we end up where we started: not story, but storytelling. *Talking It Over* and *Love, Etc.* make a little more sense if you think of them not as novels but as explorations of three modes of narration. In this view, Stuart, Oliver, and Gillian become voices rather than characters, voices whose distinctions are less psychological than semantic. Oliver represents the language novel, where the character *is* the voice and the voice *is* the story (viz., Holden Caulfield, Huck Finn, anything by Bellow or Roth), and any conflicts in plausibility are soothed over by enviably facile manipulations of language:

> The flat looked as if the *lares et penates* had done some heavy partying, and my artistic yen to reduce chaos to order being what it is, I'd stacked a few things in the sink, and was just trying to decide whether to give the Unpublished Shorter Fiction of Saltykov-Shchedrin another go or have a three-hour wank (don't be envious, only teasing), when the shrill borborygmus of the telephone alerted me to what philosophers preposterously maintain is the outside world.

In direct contrast, Stuart represents the confessional, plodding, American style, where what is confessed is as pathetic as the manner in which it's confessed, and yet somehow manages to think of itself as philosophy:

> I've come to some conclusions in my time. I'm a grown-up person, I've been an adult longer than I've been a child and

an adolescent. I've looked at the world. My conclusions may not be blindingly original, but they're still mine.

For instance, I'm suspicious of people comparing things with other things. In the days when I was more impressed with Oliver, I used to think that this mania of his proved he had not just better powers of description than I had, but also a better understanding of the world. . . . Now I think all these fancy comparisons were a way of not looking at the world. They were just distractions. And this is why Oliver hasn't changed—developed—grown up—call it what you will. Because it's only by looking at the world out there as it is and the world in here as it is that you grow up.

Gillian, finally, represents the novel as act of ventriloquism or borrowed identity (in this case, but only incidentally in Barnes' scheme, female). Again, it's an American influence, though of a decidedly more contemporary stripe than those informing Stuart and Oliver's voices. Though any number of pre-twentieth-century writers crossed gender, race, and class boundaries in their choice of character, Julian Barnes is here working in the current pre– and post–identity politics mode of demonstrating his empathic knowledge of the female psyche. Even as he cops to the fact that he's not a woman, he wants you to believe he *knows* women:

Each morning, as the girls set off for school, I kiss them and say, 'I love you.' I say it because it's true, because they should hear it and know it. I say it also for its magical powers, for its ability to ward off the world.

When did I last say it to Oliver? I can't remember. After a few years, we got into the habit of dropping the 'I'. One of us would say, 'Love you,' and the other would say, 'Love you too.' There's nothing shocking about that, nothing out of the ordinary, but one day I caught myself wondering if it weren't significant. As if you weren't taking responsibility for the feeling anymore. As if it had become somehow more general, less focused.

Two things become clear when you look at the novels in this context. The first is that Julian Barnes is a terribly smart man and a terribly, terribly skilled writer, if by smart you mean a mind that has ready access to its wide store of information and by skilled you mean a writer who can manipulate words so that they simultaneously sound familiar and original. The second is that intelligence and talent in the service of a discompassionate temperament (my thesaurus offered me as antonyms "heartless," "severe," and "cruel," but none of these is quite what I mean) are precisely the opposite of what one seeks from a novelist, or a novel. Nine out of ten book reviewers are smarter than the average novelist, which is why they're stuck writing book reviews instead of novels. One wants a novelist to be a little stupid, a little thin-skinned, and overly sensitive to the plight of his characters. Like a neurotic minor deity, a good novelist feels guilty about causing his characters to suffer so much and offers them apologies in the form of epiphanies or the satisfaction of inhabiting a meaningful narrative; but Barnes' compassion for his characters is doled out as if emotional hurts and healing could be measured as a court measures innocence and guilt or a recipe flour and sugar, and if in the end his characters fail to achieve roundness, Barnes himself fails at a far more important Forsterian dictum: he does not connect.

But then, it's hard to think of a contemporary British novelist who does. Rushdie? Not really, though Zadie Smith is doing her Oxbridge best to fix that. Ian McEwan? The man's books smell worse than newspaper wrapped around old fish. Martin Amis? Well, Martin Amis isn't really British anymore, is he? Perhaps the salient question isn't why Julian Barnes is such a bad writer, but how the current crop of British novelists managed to ruin the British novel. The idea that Julian Barnes is the successor to Laurence Sterne is nearly as unbearable as the idea that Margaret Drabble is George Eliot's heir. And how has Fielding been watered down into A.S. Byatt, and Defoe bastardized into Jeanette Winterson? At least there's Alan Hollinghurst, who is as pleasantly proficient as Forster ever was.

I don't mean to suggest that there aren't any good writers in Britain besides Hollinghurst, merely that the writers who have been anointed as the propagators of the great tradition of British fiction seem to be intent upon destroying all that's good in that tradition. Virginia Woolf thought that reading *Ulysses* was like watching a schoolboy pick his zits in public, but if her alternatives were Will Self and Tibor Fischer, perhaps even she would jump on the Julian Barnes bandwagon. Still, as far as I can tell, that makes Barnes little more than literature's wittol.

8

The Devil You Know

The Devil's Larder by Jim Crace

The difference between curiosity and promiscuity is much the same for writers as it is for lovers. The first is a good thing, the second bad, the line between the two rather blurry. At what point is inquisitiveness revealed to be a wandering eye, an inability to focus or commit?

Over the past fifteen years the British novelist Jim Crace has wooed an international audience with six clever tales about a fictitious continent, a Stone Age society, a fruit market, a shipwreck, an adolescent Jesus, and dead people. Yet each new book has had the effect of reducing rather than enlarging his oeuvre. Awards have been given, comparisons made to J.M. Coetzee, Jeanette Winterson, even Borges. These comparisons strike me as oddly apt, for Crace amplifies the worst traits of each of these great but problematic writers. He is a Coetzee for those fascinated by the pornography of perverse behavior rather than the psychology of perverse thought, a Winterson for those who pray that such thoughts can be explained away on the psychotherapist's couch, a Borges for readers who want to believe that paradoxes and labyrinths and infinity are nothing more than literary concepts. With his seventh work of fiction, *The Devil's Larder*, Crace turns his attention to gastronomy, and the result exposes him for the gourmand that he is. Rather than a David Bouley, Jim Crace stands as the Betty Crocker of contemporary novelists: though the packaging promises devil's food, angel food, German chocolate, the desiccated contents of each box taste remarkably the same.

Taken on their own, Crace's novels are inoffensive, their popularity unfortunate perhaps, but not hard to understand. As a body of work, however, their lowest-common-denominator dilettantism is the embodiment of everything I despise about contemporary fiction. This admittedly extreme opinion is not one I arrived at after reading *The Devil's Larder*, my introduction to Crace's books. Certainly *The Devil's Larder* is a slight book. Billed as "sixty-four short fictions about food," its sum is if anything less than its parts, such that one emerges from the text with little to add to the jacket description. There are sixty-four pieces; they are short (ranging from two words to ten pages); they are to the best of my knowledge fiction; and they all feature food. They are also linked by the fact that they seem to be set in the same place—the coastal village where the protagonists of *Being Dead* were murdered, perhaps, or one of the towns of his unnamed *Continent?* It's impossible to say, just as it's unclear what to make of repeated references to "Mondazy," the fictitious—and terrible—poet who is also featured in *Being Dead*. Frankly, the stories in *The Devil's Larder* defy paraphraxis, like Aesop or Lydia Davis at their insipid worst. Here is one:

He kept his curved plate in the middle of his kitchen table, with carvings on its edge. The sun, the moon, some leaves, some stars. It wasn't old or valuable, but it was natural wood, unvarnished and hand decorated. Each day, first thing, once he had done his lifts and bends, he placed his tit-bits on the plate, food to see off death. Pumpkin seeds to pro-tect the prostate. Bran for bowels. Brazil nuts for their selenium. Dried apricots. French pitted prunes. Linseed. A tomato. There were no supplements or vitamins. He had no confidence in pills. Then he drank his green-leaf tea with honey from the comb. He was a regimented man, well orga-nized, reliable. He kept his diet up, without a break, until the day he died.

Here is another:

Spitting in the omelette is a fine revenge. Or overloading it with pepper. But take care not to masturbate into the mix, as someone in the next village did, sixty years ago. The eggs got pregnant. When he heated them they grew and grew, becoming quick and lumpy, until they could outwit him (and all his hungry guests waiting with beer and bread out in the yard) by leaping from the pan with their half-wings and run-ning down the lane like boys.

Here is a third:

A migraine is a certain sign, that you should drink a case of wine. Is that confusing? No, just a lesson to be learned; that pain is fine if it's been earned by boozing.

That one is printed in fake handwriting, suggestively childish or drunken. The words are typeset in the shape of a bottle of Chianti.

These pieces remind me of only two things I've read before. The first is Jay McInerney's *Model Behavior*, an unbelievably bad collection of stories whose adolescent adventures range from the immature to the merely amateur, and whose most remarkable feature is that someone actually published it. The second is a short story sent to me by an imprisoned sex offender who had accepted Jesus Christ as his personal lord and savior; in it, a veterinarian feels guilty about euthanizing a suffering dog and is rewarded by a canine smile and wag of the dog's tail when he sends it to meet its maker. In both McInerney and the prisoner's stories, as in so much of Crace's, there can be seen the sense of discovery familiar to anyone who has ever read one of those a-ha! paragraphs that end so much fiction in college workshops: this isn't as hard as I thought! Never mind that in Crace's first story it's impossible to tell if the "carvings" adorn plate or table (syntax leans toward the former, grammar the latter); never mind that in the second the "fine revenge" lacks an object and the closing simile "like boys" prompts a similarly unanswerable question, namely, why? And never mind that in the third story the ironic "lesson" of the second half is linked to the first half by rhyme rather than reason, making it a proposition as indefensible—and unassailable—as the statement "all dogs are blue." What matters in the Cracian universe is only that the elements are arrayed in an order that resembles fiction, and that this imitation yields a simulacrum of what purports to be wisdom.

But the semblance is *too* canny. Stories like this always

bring to mind a set of "prehistoric" cave drawings found in France a few years ago. In their accurate depiction of the movement of the legs of running animals, the drawings were proved inauthentic: it wasn't until the invention of stop-motion photography that humans were able to ascertain how a horse's or deer's legs bent and lifted and came down during flight. The drawings, in other words, did not imitate life, they imitated art, and the same counterfeit status plagues the stories in *The Devil's Larder*. The short sentences masquerading as careful prose, the resonant observations which turn out to be nothing more than artless tricks of language, the use of enough irony to avoid appearing recherché: these aren't stories, but imitations of stories. My point is not merely that Crace's new book is bad, but rather that in its exclusively banal view of life, death, sex, and art, in its solemn pseudominimalist belief that any trivial detail, earnestly presented, is filled with significance, and in its reference-librarian's elevation of facts to totems, it is so bad that I began to suspect he might actually have talent. Fiction, after all, requires a monomania, the concentration to winnow away the real world until all that remains is its outline, leaving the story neatly defined by negative space. Perhaps these "short fictions" were bits of chipped stone mistakenly put on display, and Crace's Galatea lay elsewhere.

And so I read five more of his books: *Continent, The Gift of Stones, Signals of Distress, Quarantine,* and *Being Dead.* I began each one optimistically, thinking I might discover in it Crace's hidden ability or appeal. And I like Crace's subjects, like their variety and idiosyncrasy and audacity, which is why my disappointment grew greater and greater when each successive book proved as stale as *The Devil's Larder*. Look again at the story about Crace's "regimented man." The prose is detached, observational, objectifying its one-dimensional protagonist; now imagine that effect extended over two or three hundred pages. What's merely boring at 129 words is, well, *really* boring at 50,000. There's no investment in such a world, such characters, because it is not in fact a world, and they aren't actually characters; they're nothing more than shadow puppets projected on a barren wall. In fact, what I realized after reading three or four of Crace's novels is that they're not bad novels at all, but rather that they're *not* novels. They're not stories. At first I thought they were imitations of stories, but they're not even that. They're just extended metaphors Crace tries to pass off as stories.

This is a distinction I had never thought to make before. Metaphors, after all, often take the form of anecdotes, and all stories have a metaphoric rendering, usually called theme. But there is a difference. A story, as Forster brutally reduced it in *Aspects of the Novel*, is nothing more than two events separated by time, whereas a metaphor is two events separated by distance. Very often that distance is mental—is desire—but there is no desire in narrative. Time may be relentless, but not in the manner of a serial killer; it doesn't *want* to go forward, it simply goes. It isn't momentous but rather momentless, and thus the more a story seems to desire to achieve its conclusion, rather than simply arrive there, the farther it strays from its true purpose, which I'll call the accurate presentation of time. Desire in narrative is an authorial intrusion as artificial as any Barth or Barthelme hat trick. It is also human, and sacred, the age-old urge to make things make sense, to shape historical events into something more than points on a line—it's what characters do, but not writers. The speeding up that we associate with the end of a good novel represents a transformation of the character's psychology, not the writer's, the Oedipal urge to finally discover the truth, even if it destroy you. There are any number of great writers who document that urge without giving in to it themselves—Homer, for example, or Joan Didion, or Thomas Bernhard—but when a writer does give in to it the work becomes tinged with sentimentality, the cloying poetry of hymns as opposed to the ecstasy of singing voices. The god produced *deus ex machina* is, paradoxically, a god behind a wall of words that cannot begin to contain him.

For the reader, the distinction between an extended metaphor and an actual story translates to the difference between boredom and pleasure, passive observation or intellectual engagement. It's the difference between a tapestry and weaving: the former is a finished product, the relationship between its parts fixed and geometric, whereas the latter is an ongoing process that advances along ordered lines while still containing the possibility of diversion and variation—a multitude of potential tapestries, in other words, as opposed to a single scene whose very weight distorts it where it hangs on the wall, gathering dust. In an attempt to achieve that multiplicity of meaning, Crace entangles each of his so-called stories within a more or less complicated modernist framework, hoping that the act of unraveling the narrative will add what it doesn't actually contain, namely, a semblance of humanity, perhaps even your own. But Crace's juxtaposition and cross-cutting don't jar you into rethinking your position vis-à-vis what you're reading, they simply conceal or prop up the narrative's lack of spontaneity, suspense, or surprise; similarly, double-spaces and chapter breaks, the pregnant pauses of modernism, do nothing more than elide those places where characters might be expected to show something more than actorly "motivation": free will, choice. When all else fails, Crace trots out the good old direct address to the reader: "I expect you smile and brighten in expectation of some fantasy of mine." "The young man in his suit—whose name you'll know before the day is out—was left [behind]." "This is our only prayer," he writes in *Being Dead*, the conspiratorial *we* that's even more powerful—and desperate—than the gentler *you*. But when "you" bracket off these insinuations and remind yourself that "you" and Crace do not in fact form any kind of "we," "you" find yourself presented time and again with the same static picture. In six books, I never saw anything break out of the ordered mold of Crace's extended, reified metaphors. One is reminded that they are called conceits.

In his first novel, *Continent*, a kind of *Utopia*-lite, seven vignettes of an invented continent reveal a land that bears no appreciable difference to the six which already exist (Crace is apparently of the Eurasia as opposed to Europe-and-Asia school—and good for him). The worldly son of a wealthy man tells how his father sells the urine of hermaphroditic cows as magic "milk"; a man is imprisoned for speaking against the government; a visiting teacher uses the logic of topography to outrace an overconfident young buck on his horse; a scientist discovers a primitive tribe whose women go into estrus; an elderly calligrapher tells how forgeries of his work sell for thousands in the outside world; electricity comes to a rural town with comically disastrous consequences; a foreign geologist doesn't want to discover anything valuable that might lead to the destruction of an unspoiled landscape. In each case, the vignette plods toward its foreordained conclusion, its themes relentlessly borne out in every single line, its characters accruing not depth but parts, like cars on an assembly line. In Edmund White's novel *Forgetting Elena*, an older writer chastises a younger for placing a chandelier in a ballroom for no other reason than having it around to drop on the characters at the story's climax. The elements in *Continent* are similarly perfunctory, the utter redundancy of each tale never questioned. Superstition persists in the face of science, oppressive governments are bad, the tortoise always beats the hare, and so on. It takes a novel to say this?

And so on: *Being Dead* utilizes a cut-and-paste technique to elevate a pseudoscientific poetics of decay into a sort of afterlife for the otherwise uninteresting elderly couple murdered in its opening pages: they rot amid flashbacks of their past until their self-centered daughter discovers them and is sad. In its self-important presentation, Crace's tedious intercutting seems ignorant of anything written during the twentieth century. Instead, his characters remain dead, the life beaten not just from their bodies but from his flashbacks, which are nothing more than synopsis or summary, plot points for a filmscript. By contrast, *Quarantine*'s framing device is purely conceptual. This "historical" novel postulates a Jesus whose forty-day fast in the desert was a bit of adolescent drama designed to prove to disapproving parents that his faith wasn't, like, *weird*. But if you still want to, like, believe in all that God stuff, that's cool too, because after he starves to death—Jesus is a man; men can't live for forty days without food; ergo, Jesus didn't live for forty days without food—people pretend that he didn't die for various self-interested reasons, and they even pretend he worked miracles too. Is Crace attempting to disprove Christianity? Expose its hypocrisy, offer a psychological alternative to immaculate conception? It's impossible to say. Despite the fact that the narrative's central character is a boy called Jesus, he bears no relation to the historical and mythological figure of the same name, and by the same token Crace's novel fails to engage in a dialogue with the faith it's supposedly unmasking. This is not a retelling or amplification of myth; Crace is simply ignoring what's gone before. He might as well walk into a church and tell the congregation they all believe a lie. In *Signals of Distress*, a village of idiots runs around like a bunch of Tom and Jerrys for 275 pages, until a group of them gets on a ship, which then sinks. Isn't that ironic? Or unfortunate? Distressing perhaps? But hey: the announcement of the ship's sinking is typeset as though it were a photocopy of a page torn from the 1837 edition of *Oliver's Register of Ships and Shipping*. Who knows, maybe it really *is* a page from the 1837 edition of *Oliver's Register of Ships and Shipping*. Isn't that . . . isn't it *something*?

In each case, Crace's intensely sharpened focus—the man is nothing if not narrow-minded—presents a piece of the world as isolated as his regimented man with his all-natural diet, and then, through anachronism, anthropomorphism, and sleight of hand, that fragment is turned into something slightly different from what it was before, a photograph dropped from history's scrapbook and begging for an exegesis it's neither earned nor deserves—nor, more to the point, can make good on. This is because Crace refuses to admit that the novel qua novel can make a distinction between invention and reality, recorded versus lived history—in fiction, there's no such thing as nonfiction, as empirical truth, even as something to be referred to, invoked. It *all* becomes fiction. Critics often speak of the "blurred line" between fiction and nonfiction, but Crace seems not to understand that the blurriness isn't static—isn't, for that matter, a line, but rather a dialogue about the elusive goal of perfect knowledge and the imperfect tool which seeks it, the human mind. To him it's all a game: "The truth is dull and half-asleep. But lies are nimble, spirited, alive. And lying is a craft."

So says the narrator of Crace's second novel. *The Gift of Stones* is perhaps the most useful novel to examine in detail because it contains a storyteller as its central character, and as such is full of pronouncements like the above. "Of course, man must eat and food for me was earned by talk. I did invent for them another breed of tales. . . ." "When he spoke he shaped the truth, he trimmed, he stretched, he decorated. He was to truth what every stoney was to untouched flint." "You see? I've pulled a screen of grass around the story too. I'll not creep up and tell you what I saw. . . . You can be sure this is the truth— no chronicler with any sense would disappoint his listeners so."

In fact, though the foreground of this ambitious story ostensibly examines what happens when a vastly superior product (versatile, malleable bronze) is introduced into a Stone Age economy dominated by clumsy, unreliable flint implements, in the background we witness an even more radical innovation: the invention of storytelling itself. Crace is imagining the birth, as it were, of the selfsame conventions Homer would use 3,500 years later to transform a few fragments of folklore into a culture-defining myth. But where Homer wrote big, Crace writes small. Here, a literal interpretation of the term "Stone Age" creates the entire world of his novel, whose unnamed protagonist lives in a village of "the stoneys and the mongers, the villagers who dug and worked the flint, the traders who hawked and peddled it." It's unclear whether this economic stratification is meant to register as an intuitive re-creation of how life might have been lived 6,000 years ago or is simply anachronistic, but in either case life in the village seems eerily Dickensian. "You'll never guess," the protagonist says, speaking of profiteering middlemen and hardworking miners and stonemasons, "which breed was fat and wealthy, which gave the orders, which named the price, which did not stand and shiver in the line with baskets full of earth."

It is the protagonist's misfortune not only to have been born into this world as a worker rather than a capitalist, but also to lose an arm as a child. Useless as a laborer, he must find a new way to earn his keep, or at least secure handouts sufficient to his survival: he becomes a bard. It happens this way: one afternoon he sees a ship (*deus ex machina*) and follows it along the shore. He loses the ship but meets a hermit woman (*deus ex machina*) who supports herself and her daughter as a prostitute; when he returns to the village he responds to demands about where he's been with a story that his audience, though sophisticated enough to recognize his words as a mixture of truth and falseness, is nevertheless enraptured by *(deus ex machina)*. "One good story from his mouth transformed him in that village, overnight, from the wild plant, not-much-use, into their raconteur."

> And so it was that father became—not liked exactly, or respected—but useful in the village, and admired by some. . . .
> You'd meet him, too, at a great occasion, celebrating with a

tale the naming of a child or marking death and burial with some fitting yarn. And there were hardly any feasts or meetings of the village which did not feature father fantasizing at the higher table in the hall.

And—*deus ex machina*—the modern story is born, as fully formed as Athena sprung from Zeus' skull.

Note, again, the nineteenth-century inflection: the protagonist (father to the novel's narrator, who would seem to have inherited her father's skill) is neither liked nor respected but *useful.* This strikes me as the same sort of pseudorationality that Dickens lampooned Bentham for, that Huxley and Wells found so alarming in More's *Utopia.* The narrative in *The Gift of Stones* progresses with the well-oiled order of a clock's hands, but it's only believable as a blueprint for a human society if you believe in neither chance nor free will.

The protagonist returns for Doe, as he christens the woman he met on the beach, and she tells him that her husband disappeared on an errand to his village. But when the protagonist uses his newfound storytelling prowess to ask his fellow citizens about it, "they peeled away before the tale was done, unmoved by father's portrait of the widow and her child on the heath. . . . My father stood alone and startled—for now he understood the power of the truth." But what is that power? And how has it worked? Why are the villagers interested—willing to pay for—one story but not the other? If they were somehow responsible for the husband's disappearance one could attribute their lack of interest to guilt, but that doesn't appear to be the case. The only thing that comes close to providing an answer is, again, anachronism: the villagers' taste runs toward inconsequential fantasy rather than heavier stuff, just like today's fickle, fainthearted media consumers. *Deus ex machina.* Crace's story makes his point too conveniently, too simplistically; it exists not only without nuance but without alternative, and as such is a reductive look at both his invented world and the real world it's supposedly commenting on. And it doesn't affect anything anyway: Doe continues to work as a prostitute with the men of the village as her clientele and the narrator continues to tell stories until, conveniently enough, another ship returns, discharging sailors who kill Doe with an arrow tipped by the bronze implement promised in the jacket copy. Within a page, bronze tools are everywhere—the kind of market saturation Bill Gates would kill for—and the villagers abandon their quarries, presumably in hopes of finding a place far away from the dreaded innovation. And as they embark on their great trek into—or away from?—the past, they turn to the protagonist "to invent a future for us all."

Here, again, is the a-ha! moment of the tiny tales in *The Devil's Larder*, the same messianic urge that lurks behind *Quarantine* and *Being Dead*. History disappears beneath memory's distortions; only perception remains. So one might as well have a story that tidies things up, that inspires hope, right? Fiction is a balm, a sop even. On bad days, when everything I write seems inconsequential or meaningless, I've thought as much, but I'm not sure Crace allows fiction even that much life. What little compassion I'd had for his work disappeared when I read the following interview with him in *Bookforum:*

> People are baffled when they hear me prefer journalism over fiction. But I'm equally baffled that anyone could inspect the

array of subjects highlighted by serious newspapers, note the size and variety of their readerships, consider the role they play in providing the source material of our opinions, and still consider the literary novel an equal force. Of course, narrative literature increases in importance when newspapers don't or aren't allowed to do their job. I couldn't argue that Russian newspapers of the cold war period represent a better record of their times than the novels of Pasternak or Solzhenitsyn, for example. And narrative literature can be immensely important among communities that are marginalized or misrepresented by newspapers. I could make a good case for the gay novel, the black novel, the feminist novel of the last fifty years. But these are novels with alert constituencies as well as plain readers. Now, step back, consider me, consider Britain. A white, middle-aged, heterosexual male in a bourgeois, liberal democracy. Where is my constituency? How can my thin novels, with their overload of rhythmic metaphors and their few thousand readers, claim equal importance with newspapers? Poets (and novelists) are "the unacknowledged legislators of the world"? Not anymore, they're not. Come on, you self-deluding writers, get a grip!

This is perhaps the most damning confession I've ever seen a novelist make. It's not simply a statement of bad faith, but an admission that he has *no idea* what a novel is, what a novel does. The problem with most contemporary novelists is that they seem to have forgotten the basic ontological difference between history and fiction—that one is real and the other made up—and write their smug "realist" novels with no indication of the unbridgeable gap that separates their flights of fancy from the horrific trajectories of actual aircraft. Crace, admirably, doesn't pretend to record history in his novels. But he does seem to think that the measure of any narrative's "importance"—and by importance he means usefulness—is its ability to do so. And so, convinced before he sets out that his novels can't "claim equal importance" with newspapers, he allows fact and fiction to dissolve into each other like sugar in water, leaving a sticky residue on everything they touch. This is just another variation of the inferiority complex felt by a select group of contemporary novelists—all that bleating by David Foster Wallace and Jonathan Franzen about their lack of connection to that thing they call "the culture"—but which, on examination, turns out to be nothing more than a denigration of fiction for not being something it was never meant to be. And trotting out poor Shelley to defend your opinion is just an insult to the poet's memory, not to mention the kind of literal-mindedness that ought to disqualify one from being a poet (or a novelist). For a man who writes nothing but metaphors, Crace is clueless as to how they work.

So look. I'm not, at this late date, going to suggest that fiction is or isn't as important as history. That's a question for metaphysics (or a novel). All I want to point out is that fiction doesn't record history, or compete with it. Fiction interprets history. It was, in fact, history that originally aspired to fiction, not the other way around. "What happened" was considered less important than something we'd now call "spin"; what made *The Iliad*, for example, so vital to its listeners wasn't its truth value, perceived or actual, but rather its ability to tell its listeners what it meant to be Greek, a lesson so historically resonant that everyone from Virgil to Dante to Dos Passos has used it as a model for what fiction can aspire to. It wasn't until Suetonius began writing his biographies of the Caesars around the first century CE that objectivity and subjectivity began to separate into two distinct genres, the former reifying itself into history, the latter mutating through any number of forms into what we call, inadequately, vaguely, fiction. Like Potter Stewart and pornography, I can't tell you what fiction is, but I know it when I see it. Fiction doesn't make meaning by reifying ideas, because you can't reify something that doesn't exist. Rather, it vests meaning in a series of contextual relationships: writer and reader, invented and actual, shapely narrative and shapeless history. Ultimately, fiction speaks to the narrativizing heart in all of us while gently admonishing that history has no such neatness, none of the inevitabilities of climax, resolution, and dénouement that religion or politics or art comforts us with. The novelist treats the facts of history as a juggler treats his balls rather than as a rock climber treats his pitons: it's the amount of time he can keep away from them that's most fascinating, not the time he spends clinging on for dear life. The novelist doesn't tell lies. He unmasks the truth. He doesn't provide sheltering illusions. He dispels them. If Jim Crace, former journalist, thinks journalism does something more important than this, then he should get on a plane to Kabul right now. He'll have to hurry if he wants to make it before the shooting's over.

POSTSCRIPT, November 16, 2001: Crace has written one other novel, *Arcadia*, but it's out of print and by the time I'd tracked it down and had it mailed to me I was simply too weary to read it for this review. What can I say? God save the USPS.

9

American Booty

Don't the Moon Look Lonesome by Stanley Crouch

1.

Sometimes a bad novel is a gift. This is particularly evident when that novel is written by a writer as ambitious as Stanley Crouch. Here is a book with much to say about three of our culture's most important social and literary themes—race, art, and love; and, when one has sifted through the bombast and the clumsiness to the truisms that lurk at the heart of this fat book like minnows in a deep and muddy river, one does see what's wrong with American society in general and American literature in particular. For lack of a better term, I'm going to call that problem false pretenses. If only chronology were irrelevant to judgment, and the novel its subject rather than its words: then *Lo's Diary* would be just as good as *Lolita*, and *Don't the Moon Look Lonesome* would be as important as *Invisible Man*.

Not since Donna Tartt's "muse and Maecenas" to Paul Ed-

ward McGloin has a novel started with such a grand dedication: "For Albert Murray, Ralph Ellison, and Saul Bellow, men-
tors all." *The Secret History* at least had the distinction of being
a well-written thriller; but *Don't the Moon Look Lonesome* is neither well-written nor thrilling. In fact, the novel is essentially
plotless, being concerned with issues rather than stories, the
primary issue being the thesis that we are all different yet all
the same, so get over it already.

Crouch's subjects are African- and occasionally other
Americans; music, mainly jazz, but music in Crouch's world
seems representative of the ideal state of art; and interracial
heterosexuality, specifically the black-man-on-top-of-white-
woman variety, oh my. The white woman, an aspiring jazz
singer named Carla, is the protagonist of the novel, but it is
more useful to think of her as the moon of the novel's title, the
lone spot of white in a vast field of blackness. For Carla is less
an aspiring anything than a figure resembling Norman
Mailer's mythical white Negro of a few decades ago. She
doesn't just sing black, she also dates black, befriends black,
cooks black, and, best of all, looks black—at least, as far as her
boyfriend is concerned, where it counts: "In the black night of
their home Maxwell always endeared himself to her when she
lay naked on her stomach and he slowly rubbed and gently
squeezed her backside while whispering, 'I know my dog by the
way he barks, I know my baby from the feeling in the dark.' "

Maxwell doesn't always speak in couplets, nor does Crouch
always write in them (or, I should say, quote in them, since
Crouch's couplets, like his title, are borrowed from jazz songs).
But pairs and polarities in this novel about race (in Crouch's
America there are only two races which matter, in much the

same way that television has the Big Three and then those other networks) are more than a little in evidence, most notably in the person of Carla—who, it turns out, is a woman possessed of an "anatomical anomaly." To put it as bluntly as a friend of Maxwell's does, she's "a blonde with a black ass."

This information must be given its context. Here is the order of facts presented to us about Carla: we learn first, that she is white; second, that she has a black boyfriend; third, that problems have arisen in the relationship because of this discrepancy in skin tone; fourth, that "couldn't nobody tell [she] was white if all they got to see was the shadow of her profile"; fifth, that she has enjoyed Negro music since her girlhood days as "a local skating whiz who showed Olympic potential"; and sixth, that she is an aspiring jazz singer. In short, she is a step above a talking Barbie; she actually sleeps with her black friend, as opposed to hanging out with him in the Malibu beach house.

But the dozens of references to Carla's gigantic boody— Crouch's spelling; I always use a "t" myself—do more than eroticize her. They embody a theme that Crouch first articulated a few years ago in *The All-American Skin Game*, namely, that "the grand shindig of American civilization" is a product of miscegenation. And so race, far from being a hindrance in love, is the ideal way to spice up the pot. In life, who can say? But in this novel, we have only the evidence that the author provides, and those clues seem to lead to the following conclusion: Carla's whiteness is in fact irrelevant to her relationship with Maxwell, because it isn't real—the only thing white about Carla is her "mannish" Aryan sister, preparing for the "race war" out there in Ohio, and you can be sure her ass is as flat as

Twiggy's—and because Carla has already submitted to black culture in the most primal sense. Boyfriend Maxwell, at any rate, is possessed of "the conqueror's spirit," which is to say, he is "not the kind of man who can feel comfortable under a woman," a fact that Carla acknowledges explicitly.

"Carla . . ."

"Yes, sweetheart."

"You know you couldn't hold me if I didn't want you to hold me."

"I know."

"But I would have had to hurt you, baby."

"Yes, you would. Right here."

"I love you too much for that."

"I know that. Maxwell . . ."

"Yes, baby."

"Oh, I don't know. I just love you. I just love you so much."

So Carla has submitted to her man. But to what end? In lieu of a love that is testified to but never witnessed, what we are left with is music. Maxwell is a tenor saxophonist, further along in his career than Carla, and, like her last boyfriend, the dead drummer Bobo, he uses his "horn" to "intimidate" Carla, and so bring her to a deeper understanding of her art:

Soaking in rhythm and stroking it and coming to know herself through it was what she had done—each ounce of her body carrying and sending the beat, from her big toes all the way under to the heels of her feet and up her ankles, then her legs, around the horn of her behind, up her spine and shoul-

ders, scaling the vertebrae of her neck, the round back of her
head, across the scalp, down her forehead, zooming off her
nose, swinging back to her lips, gliding on down to her chin,
dropping to her breast bone, then to each of her full but not
heavy breasts, moving onto her belly, the beat crossing the
pubic thatch that guarded her lower lips until . . .

until just when you think Crouch is finally going to give
his readers a taste of the miscegenated shindig they have
awaited for more than three hundred pages,

that beat disappeared through the invincible space between
her vagina and the tops of her thighs: that concave cupping
of air, never less than open, regardless of how close she held
her legs together.

This passage is perhaps the most literal evocation of the rhythm
method I've ever encountered. It's so fascinatingly Jungian that
it's hard to put down, a true rape of anima by animus; but not
even this juggernaut of phallocentric conceit can hide the fact
that Crouch, for all his declarations in support of assimilation, is
less interested in the union of black and white than in the inability of white people to consummate that union. From the back
there is that sterile "Negroid boody," from the front a decoy
vagina in which Maxwell's seed is continually wasted. And yet
there is no hint of blame in Crouch's descriptions: here is Carla,
ready for whatever her man has to give, even pain.

In his essays, Crouch repeatedly insists that "black Americans have had to scale, bore through, or detonate the prejudicial walls that blocked access to the banquet of relatively

unlimited social advancement that we acknowledge as the grand inspirational myth of American life," a mixed metaphor of such bland grandiosity (barbarians at the gates, a place at the table, I have a dream) that it raises suspicion in the reader's mind. But it is his fiction that reveals Crouch's vision of American history to be, just like his women, full of holes. For whatever the coupling of black and white, the very nature of the union renders the product sterile and ungainly as a mule.

2.

Of course there is a plot. Stanley Crouch, like other social critics who treat fiction as an appendix to their field, has resorted to realism, because realism, like social criticism, is seen to lend itself to the reductive, instructive narrative. The reduction is that Carla is afraid Maxwell will leave her because she is white, but he doesn't leave her. The instruction is that it would be wrong for Maxwell to leave Carla as a consequence of her skin color, because race shouldn't interfere with love.

It's hard to render the story more fully than that. There are set pieces—a trip to Houston to visit Maxwell's parents; the return to New York City; bouts of drinking in various bars in various cities—but these diversions are almost wholly unrelated to the development of the characters and the relationship between them. Thus, on the second page of the novel we are told that after five years together "everything the two knew about the other had become secondary to his being black and her being white," but four hundred pages later all we've learned is that Maxwell is "still sliding away." It takes another twenty

pages before we learn that Maxwell had heretofore been "above
the silly aspects of race, but in that last year before they trav-
eled to visit [his parents], he began hanging out with a different crowd." This "different crowd" is never seen, but it is
presumably under their tutelage that

> instead of being philosophical about on-duty cabs passing
> him up, or calmly telling off white people who tried to step
> in front of him in lines, Maxwell became extremely angry,
> returning home with one tale after another of how tired he
> was of eating shit just because his skin was dark. He started
> using some of those clichés that he used to make fun of, that
> "us versus them" philosophy that usually demanded certain
> kinds of ethnic costumes and body oils and hairstyles in
> order to make the clear point that these Americans were nei-
> ther white people nor black people who had been overcome
> by white society. They were not anybody's black Anglo-
> Saxons. Or so they thought. To her dismay, especially since
> she was still dreaming of having a child, Maxwell sneered
> about the "almost niggers," "the not quite niggers," the "I-
> wish-I-was niggers" who had been so bleached out inside
> that their skin was just a husk, an ethnic mirage. They were
> black on the outside but corny as Kansas in the summertime.
> The contempt he showed for such people in his conversation
> when they appeared on television or in restaurants or came
> up to him asking for an autograph after a performance was
> incrementally frightening. It was as if, out of nowhere, he
> began to accept some old-fashioned idea about the complete
> separateness of black and white.

This paragraph, with its cobbled-together "clichés" and "old-
fashioned ideas," comes 427 pages into a 530-page novel, and it

is the closest thing we get to illustration or explanation of Maxwell's "sliding away," a slide that continues for another seventy pages or so with phrases such as "and on it went," and "for a while," until "out of nowhere"—and in a phone call, no less—a contrite Maxwell declares that "Ezekiel did not raise me to turn and run from the woman I love. Not for no niggers, not for no crackers, not for no dadgum body." When Carla asks what had caused him to become concerned about her race in the first place—perhaps she, like the reader, is wondering what shadow conflict has been endured and overcome—all Maxwell says is, "I wanted to be something somebody was telling me to be"; but that "somebody" is as elusive as the "different crowd" that he's been "hanging out with," as hard to pin down as "these Americans" and "such people" and the ever-present "they" who people Maxwell's " 'us-versus-them' philosophy." But no matter. "Her loneliness had been put on hold. Ooo, ooo, ooo: what a little mush on a moonstruck night will do." Crouch's couplets, you see, tend to appear when there's a point to be made—or, rather, missed.

But to focus on plot would be to miss the point along with him. Plot is only a skeleton in the modern novel, and a fragile one at that, right? As in *Ulysses*—whose banner headlines from the Telegraph Office chapter Crouch borrows for a set piece on a Negro church service—the flesh and blood of this novel are its diversions, almost all of which appear as recollections, "the marching legions of memory as they came to attack or rescue or soothe or mystify." Thus we are treated to multipage descriptions of music ("His melodies might be long balletic bounds of sustained notes that sailed up over the meter"; "the drummer . . . had a sexy little triplet bouncing off of his snare that made her feel as if she were being patted on the ass") or art

("The flowers on canvas could lift you into the region of spiritual confidence that radiates from beauty so pure one would think those brushstrokes could turn a jar of piss into apple juice"; "it was a one-to-one relationship made successful or a failure by a third factor, that painter just as alone as Daniel Boone shouting at the top of a valley"). Often these descriptions are couched in faux-Platonic dialogues between tongue-loosened drunks; and these dialogues allow Crouch to make even more preposterous pronouncements than he could in his own voice. For example, the origin of misogyny: "The moment in bed. That's where misogyny starts: when a guy goes through all of that and the pussy's not shit." For example, homosexuality and the abuse of freedom: "There were naked men with bleeding feet hoisted up from the floor and held by chains that formed seats from which their asses hung out. On the floor were cans of Crisco. Men would scoop out the right amount of Crisco and rub it on their forearms and the backs of their hands. Then they would push their fists up the rectums of the men sitting in the seats of the chains." For example, gridlock, Judaism, and the politics of guilt tripping: "You sweat through that and the fucking pollution of all those cars making you feel like you know something, a little bit anyway, about the gas chambers some of these Jews always use as an I've-been-fucked-over-more-than-you credit card." And, of course, race relations, and Crouch's particular fascination with miscegenation: "the white boys who imitated the swaggering simian moves and gestures, bad taste, and worse behavior of rappers"; "these black kids wearing the false faces in a carnival of street niggerism . . . played into the hands of racists, or with all their adolescent energy, created so much disgust and fear, they helped breed racism"; "she was still full of that special sass and vinegar too many lost when they climbed up into the penthouse. No deracinated Negress was she."

I could go on, but why? Suffice it to say that here is one black man calling other black men monkeys, denying blackness to those African Americans who fail to live up to his standards and conferring it on those who do. All this from a writer who has proclaimed that American fiction should represent a "far, far richer sense of the inner lives that give our nation its particular complexity." This sentiment is grossly belied by Crouch's own attempt at rendering that "far, far richer sense." One closes *Don't the Moon Look Lonesome* with less sense of its characters' inner lives than of its author's need to swing back and forth between the roles of assimilationist peacemaker and agent provocateur. By which I mean that when I read Crouch's dismissal of Malcolm X's "absolutely inaccurate juxtaposition" of house niggers and field niggers in *The All-American Skin Game*, I couldn't *help* but think of that old adage about the pot and the kettle.

3.

Let's be blunt for a moment. *Don't the Moon Look Lonesome* is a terrible novel, badly conceived, badly executed, and put forward in bad faith; reviewing it is like shooting fish in a barrel, and it wouldn't even be worth the effort had it been written by someone other than the National Book Critics Circle Award–nominated "frequent panelist" on *The Charlie Rose Show*, a figure variously described as "a jazz virtuoso of the

American essay" by Tom Wolfe and "an embodiment . . . of
hard-earned integrity" by Henry Louis Gates Jr. "Reading
him," blurbs Pauline Kael, "is like watching a sharpshooter—
when he misses, it adds to the showmanship." In fact his most
recent book of essays, *Always in Pursuit*, is decorated by no
fewer than eleven such endorsements, and yet there is an un-
dertone to all that praise ("hard-earned"; "when he misses";
"you don't have to agree with him"; "however"), a qualification,
almost an apology for the endorsed product, and even a sample
reading of the essays reveals why. For Crouch is neither virtuosic nor possessed of good marksmanship; he's just another
demagogue in an age that confuses demagoguery with honesty,
a black man who uses the veil of an anti-p.c. polemic to make
criticisms of black culture that white Americans are either too
cowed or too smart to put forth themselves. This doesn't mean
Crouch is always or even often wrong, although he's wrong
often enough; rightness or wrongness has less to do with
Crouch's agenda than getting a rise, scoring points, gaining
status in a manner that seems eerily similar to that of gangsta
rappers. But Crouch's posturing strikes me as less sophisticated than that of the current generation of black musicians he
so loathes. Rap's iconography and lexicography present a romanticized version of ghetto life to its white audience while simultaneously appropriating, inflating, and parroting the
trappings of bourgeois wealth to its black fans, and if you think
that's lame then compare it to Crouch's scorecarding of good
Negroes (Albert Murray, Ralph Ellison, Johnnie Cochran), bad
(James Baldwin, Toni Morrison, Christopher Darden), and the
occasional fence-straddler (Richard Wright, O.J. Simpson).
For, though Crouch writes exclusively about black culture, his

message, like Maxwell's transcendental "beat," is intended for whites only.

This is a writer who calls Toni Morrison's novels "bottles of bathtub corn liquor." He calls James Baldwin wrongheaded, a "professional Negro" who "engages" by "harangue," "selling out to hysterical alienation by so overstating the case that the issue is smudged beyond recognition." He calls his own novel "a whopper," and although I assume he meant it in the sense of "a large fish," his wording—"bringing this whopper on home"—puts one in mind of that other fast-food chain's auto-mated request: "You want fries with that?" All this from some-one who is, to borrow a phrase Eliot Weinberger used to describe Robert Bly, "a windbag, a sentimentalist, a slob in the language," a writer who plays fast and loose with words, if not simply the truth, while simultaneously exempting himself from examination by accusing his enemies of the tactics he uses himself.

Implicit in this posturing is a canonical self-presentation ("This, my second book of essays, is dedicated to my mother, Emma Bea Crouch, who died a few years ago on Blooms-day, symbolizing for me the essential role she had played in my development as a writer") that rests less on a sense of per-sonal space than on what Crouch, like almost every writer since Zora Neale Hurston, has called the "lyricism of black Ameri-can culture." In an essay on Albert Murray in *Always in Pur-suit*, Crouch quotes his subject's observation that "no other people in the land have as yet evolved a characteristic idiom that reflects a more open, robust, and affirmative disposition toward diversity and change. Nor is any other idiom more smoothly geared to open-minded improvisation. Moreover, never has improvisation been more conditioned by esthetic values." This is a declaration that reeks of professional jingoism of the type Crouch sees in Baldwin and his heirs. In such a vision, a black person's every utterance is both a moral pronouncement and an aesthetic event, and to fail at it is somehow to fail at being black. And yet here is a writer who says that someone "experienced extreme anger" instead of got mad. His characters are always "answering in the affirmative" instead of just saying yes, possibly as part of the effort of "maintaining intimacy"; and they can't even glance at the FDR Drive without remembering that it was "named after the man who had supplied the money for the Triborough [Bridge] to be finished and had put many New Yorkers back to work during the Depression by federally financing all manner of building."

More serious, though, is the sentimental sleight of hand that characterizes his polemic. Crouch's method is to attack various generalities—Malcolm X's categories of house and field slaves; W.E.B. Du Bois' notion of an African American as a person with two souls, "one American, one Negro"—with the classic one-two of slippery discourse. He first dismisses them as generalities, which they clearly are, and then he makes the general statement that these and other tropes have no basis in reality, which they clearly do. This is essentially the rhetoric of political speechifying, and for the life of me I've never been able to figure out why readers succumb to it over and over again, besides the fact that the effort of refuting it reduces you to a nitpicking pedantry that can drive you *insane.*

Still, for the sake of thoroughness, let's consider one example, from the essay on Albert Murray quoted earlier. In this essay, Crouch is presumably explaining the way Northerners view Southern violence:

> The relationship of pride to bloodlust was transmuted into the vision of mad gallantry that took John Brown to Harper's Ferry and made possible those reckless attacks by Confederate troops that resulted in the green fields turned red by the gore of defeat, defeat at the hands of Yankees, Midwestern farm boys and Northern kids scooped up out of the cities, all backed up by the indispensable help of the Negro, whose freedom was the issue of that war in the first place. The South is where most of the Civil War battles were fought and where Washington, D.C., is located. So we too frequently see the South as a place of dislocation and barbarism, imbecility and decadence. We, presumptively perched in the alto and soprano reaches of the nation, look upon Southerners, the residents of the bass clef, with a mix of pity and contempt.

Now, John Brown was a Northerner, born in Ohio and first attaining historical prominence with the door-to-door murder of five pro-slavery men in Kansas. And when Robert E. Lee attacked the fort that Brown held at Harper's Ferry in 1859, it was Lee—then still in the employ of the only American government in existence—who won, and had Brown hanged. What "mad gallantry" and "recklessness" had to do with either side's actions is unclear. If Crouch's point is that John Brown somehow started the War of the Rebellion, as Northerners called it at the time, then he's off by two years and is rendering history as simplistically as when he says that freeing the slaves "was the issue of the war." Lincoln never hid his motivation for declaring war ("If I could save the Union without freeing any slave I would do it . . ."); his Emancipation Proclamation did not even apply to slaves in those states (Delaware, Maryland, Kentucky, and Missouri) that had not joined the Confederacy, and in fact one of the prime motivating factors in the Proclamation was the hope that it would deter Southern slaves from helping their masters in what the Virginia grandfather of a friend of mine called the War of Northern Aggression to his dying day. In fact, most of the battles of what was also called the War Between the States, the War of Secession, and the War for Southern Independence did take place in the South, just as most of the battles in World War II took place in Europe, but why the South should be rendered "a place of dislocation and barbarism, imbecility and decadence" while the North is the birthplace of all the ideas "that were expanded and refined in order to adjust to the intricacies of human experience, action, conflict, and ambition within these United States" is, like so much else in this single paragraph, unclear.

And then, finally, there is that closing metaphorical conceit about the "alto and soprano reaches of the nation" looking down upon "the residents of the bass clef," for sideways comment on which I turn to Philip Roth:

> "What about when I say the writer should be restrained from spilling the beans before they are digested? What about *that?*"
>
> Zuckerman the satirist remained silent.
>
> "That stinks too?" asked Pepler. "Don't condescend to me, *tell* me!"
>
> "Of course it doesn't 'stink.'"
>
> "*But?*"

"But it's straining, isn't it, for an effect?" As serious and uncondescending a man of letters as there could ever be, Zuckerman said, "I wonder if it's worth the effort."

4.

This Pepleresque use of metaphorical conceit is the most often repeated stylistic construction Crouch uses in both his polemical writing and his fiction, starting with the dedication page ("TO JUDY JOYCE, whose knowledge of food service and sailing helped me caulk the hull of one chapter") to the last paragraph of the last page of the novel ("The emotion that those tunes allowed her to free nearly lifted Carla up off the floor and sent the girl from South Dakota safely sailing out of the window, like the very first dinosaur who ever learned how to use her wings"). It is difficult to figure out why exactly, especially given the strange places that these sentences tend to end up. Dinosaurs? Learning to use their wings? And this relates to Carla's happiness *how?* My hunch is that it has something to do with the fact that Crouch's book is subtitled "a novel in blues and swing." Something to do with jazz, in other words, which is somehow made an ancillary subject to every topic Crouch has written on, from Ellison to O.J.; something to do with improvisation, which Crouch has elsewhere declared as "very important to my vision of life in our time." In fact, "important" doesn't begin to capture his feelings on the subject: "I believe that one of the central intellectual shortcomings of American life is the fact that so little has been done with the flexible profundity of jazz metaphor."

And so we come to what might possibly be the one justifiable raison d'être for this novel—not theme, not narrative, not sex, not politics, but aesthetics, specifically an improvisational jazz aesthetic Crouch believes is "not only about transforming pulp frogs, [but] also about slaying the dragon and making cuisine out of his corpse" (the dragon, by the way, is "our industrial world," and if that doesn't clear things up, I'm sorry, I don't get it either). In essay after essay, Crouch carries the torch for jazz, calling it not only the greatest American musical form—which seems as safely uncontestable as his assertion that "black Americans have had to scale, bore through, or detonate . . . prejudicial walls"—but also a potential source of inspiration for all the arts, a model for all that is good, true, beautiful. But Crouch is right: jazz hasn't had the kind of ramifying cultural impact lesser art forms have had, and the same is true of the notions of improvisation and individuality he sees as metaphorically attendant upon it.

To some degree, Crouch's question begs its own answer. After all, what aspect of composition *isn't* improvisation? Don't we make it all up, from narrative to character to the sentences and the metaphors we use to describe them? And he seems to be missing another obvious point: writing isn't music. It isn't performed. Novels, unlike scores, can't be interpreted, can't be improvised once printed. A novel, even more than a painting or sculpture, which can deteriorate with time, is the most reified of all art forms—a point poignantly rendered in Nabokov's "Lolita, Lolita, Lolita, Lolita, Lolita, Lolita, Lolita, Lolita. Repeat till the page is full, printer."

Turning the novel into a jazz composition would require more than Crouch's formal, uh, innovation, which, though it aims to connote freedom, spontaneity, and improvisation,

comes across as merely unrevised. It would require an interme-
diary figure between reader and writer, a performer who not
only adds inflection and emphasis, but also has the freedom to
change words as he sees fit, shuffle sentences, move paragraphs
around. Perhaps he would end this particular book on a more
realistic note, or cut out the middle four hundred pages, since
they do little more than repeat themselves over and over again.

But there is a deeper problem inherent in Crouch's use of
the metaphor. Crouch claims to believe in improvisation, but
what he really believes in is idiosyncrasy—that is, individuality; and when this notion is examined further, it becomes clear
that what Crouch really believes in is The Individual, the one to
whom all other individuals should aspire. In other words, jazz
is an improvisational musical form encouraging individual expression on the bandstand, but a belief in jazz culture is a codi-
fied and largely dated way of life—which is why all those
references to cool cats and jive turkeys in Baldwin now make us
wince. Charlie Parker was an individual, but all those jazzmen
who play in the style of Bird are not. Ralph Ellison was an individual; Stanley Crouch, his student, is not. Crouch claims to be
inventing a new kind of writing, but the truth is he's just itch-
ing to join the club. And when he says his new writing is a jazz
derivative, "a novel in blues and swing," what he's really doing
is using Hurston's "lyricism of black American culture" as a
way of deflecting examination—criticize me, and you criticize
black culture—a pose which, though less blunt than the letter-
writing campaign protesting the neglect of Toni Morrison for
the National Book Award in 1987, is no less political, and no
closer to actual questions of quality.

In art as in life: people admire the *idea* of individuality, of newness, more than they admire the new and individual thing itself. The truth is, humans look for the familiar in all things, the psychic extension of the comforts of home. Food, art, politics. But humans are also fickle and get bored easily and unexpectedly, and, as Crouch points out, one of jazz's strengths is its ability to maintain the tension between the familiar and the strange; perhaps the closest writing comes to this is in the regurgitative, recyclical nature of literary criticism, which might explain why certain critical works—*Sexual Personae* comes to mind, as does *Tradition and the Individual Talent*, and, rather pointedly in Crouch's case, *The Anxiety of Influence*—assume a popularity that overshadows the work they describe. In his writing Crouch seems to be burning the candle at both ends, to no avail: his critical work on Ralph Ellison and Albert Murray has, in the case of the former, added nothing to our knowledge, and, in the case of the latter, done nothing to galvanize either Murray's or Crouch's reputations; and so he's decided to follow in the pater's footsteps and turn to fiction. It's all very *Anxiety of Influence*, very ambitious, very big. In fact bigness may be the point, because *every fucking artist in America* feels the need to make a big statement right now (even me). Alas, we live in an age that confuses pretentiousness for ambition (*Magnolia* as opposed to *Boogie Nights*), lauds intention over accomplishment (*Underworld* as opposed to *White Noise*), and can't distinguish between condescension and charity (*Pulp Fiction* as opposed to *Jackie Brown*); and this condition seems to dovetail neatly into the view of art embodied in Crouch's novel, which is heroic and Romantic—hot, in other words, just like a jazz club. For here is a onetime jazz critic whose moonlighting role as race provocateur became his full-time job (but let's not forget "you don't have to agree with him to learn from him"). Now he's posing as a novelist, a bardic instructor, a lyrical teacher of lessons. But as far as I can tell, the only useful lesson that Crouch's novel reminds us of is this: in fiction, unlike life, you can't fake it. That must be hard for Crouch; the pose is part of his manner, just as it is in rap, and it's a shame that what works on *60 Minutes* and MTV doesn't cut it on the page.

But, finally, let us not lose sight of the fact that Stanley Crouch's transgressions are against the laws of man rather than the universe, and, mercifully, culture changes. What's a sin today is a faux pas tomorrow, and tomorrow's faux pas won't even register the day after. While I'm sure there are still people who condemn interracial relationships, I doubt many of them will be reading this novel, and so it is that in response to this novel's title's question one wants finally to answer "No," simply, wearily, but also sternly. "It *doesn't.*"

10

The Moody Blues

The Black Veil: A Memoir with Digressions by Rick Moody

Rick Moody is the worst writer of his generation.

I apologize for the abruptness of this declaration, its lack of nuance, of any meaning besides the intuitive: *so what you're saying is this guy really sucks, huh?* But as I made my way through Moody's oeuvre during the past few months I was unable to come up with any other starting point for this review. Or, more accurately, every other starting point I tried felt disingenuous, nothing more than a way of setting Moody up in order to knock him down. One of those starting points: "Rick Moody is a lot of things but he's not actually dumb." This was supposed to be an attempt at charity, and though I still think it's true enough, I don't think it matters; at any rate, it doesn't make up for the badness of his books. Another attempt: "In his breakthrough novel *The Ice Storm*, Rick Moody evinces a troubling fascination with adolescent sexual organs which is partially explained in his latest book, *The Black Veil*, a so-called 'memoir with digressions.'" Again, the observation strikes me as correct. The problem here was in assuming that what most readers think of as the subject of a story has any role in a Moody project beyond giving his tangled prose something to wrap itself around, the same way a vine will wrap itself around the nearest thing to hand, be it trellis, tree, or trash. Yet another false start: *"The Black Veil* is the worst of Rick Moody's very bad books."* Here the first mistake was in focusing on the books themselves, which bear the same relationship to Moody's career as his subjects do to his prose: the former come across as little more than a prop for the latter, incidental, interchangeable. Additionally, *Garden State*, Moody's debut—despite his citing "the proposition put forth by a vocal minority: that *Garden State* is my best novel"—is, in fact, even worse than *The Black Veil*, and *"The Black Veil* is the second worst of Rick Moody's very bad books" just doesn't have the same ring to it.

So. Stop reading here if you're looking for an objective or, for that matter, rational dissection of the work of Hiram Frederick Moody III. At this point, the use of the diminutive Rick is about the only wise decision I'm willing to give him credit for. The plain truth is that I've stared at pages and pages of Moody's prose and they remain as meaningless to me as the Korean characters which paper the wall of a local restaurant. Actually, that comparison's not particularly apt, because I know the Korean writing means *something*, but I'm not convinced Moody's books are about anything at all. In fact, it's only when I consider *The Black Veil* stripped of any pretense to content that I can ascribe it a measure of objecthood—not as the diagnostic, hermeneutical genealogy it purports to be, but rather as the latest in what I've come to think of as a series of imitations or echoes of Moody's more talented, or at any rate more authentically individual, peers. Seen in this light, *The Black Veil* is Moody's attempt at *A Heartbreaking Work of Staggering Genius*, *Purple America* Moody's version of *Infinite Jest*, *The Ice Storm* his take on *The Virgin Suicides*, and *Garden State* a pastiche of various New Narrative writers who published in *Between C and D* in the eighties. No doubt Moody is even now at work on a sprawling "social novel" à la *The Corrections*; given his rate of output—six books in a decade—we can probably expect to see it in stores by the end of next year, just in time for Christmas.

Together these books amount not so much to an oeuvre as to a career, one whose success, though fascinating, is entirely inexplicable to me. In fact, I have to confess I consider myself unequal to the task of analyzing Moody's writing. Its faults strike me as uniform and self-evident and none complex enough for a sustained analysis; my gut feeling is that if you honestly don't believe it's bad then you're part of the problem. When I finished *The Black Veil* I scrawled "Lies! Lies! All lies!" on the cover and considered my job done. Like all of his books, it is pretentious, muddled, derivative, bathetic. His much-touted compassion strikes me as false (in his fiction he makes his characters suffer in order to solicit your pity, and this seems no less true of the self he describes in *The Black Veil*); his equally praised prose—"rhythmic," "evocative" and "musical" are the tags you see most often—comes only at the expense of precision, which is to say, of truth. Further, as Moody's career has progressed, his books have striven to be more mythic and more postmodern and more real all at the same time, so it is perhaps not surprising that his latest endeavor is a work of hagiography masking itself as self-lacerating autobiography. *The Black Veil* asks us to consider its subject—the aforementioned Hiram Frederick Moody III, aka Rick—as a postmodern tragic hero, ironic as well as iconic, America's Battered Inner Child–cum–Messianic Storyteller. Every page practically cries out: *love me despite my flaws.*

Well, I don't. Perhaps that's a failure of empathy on my part, or an indication that I'm not the intended audience for Moody's musings. But as I puzzled my way through this and the rest of Moody's books I found myself looking not for the place in their execution or conception where they went wrong, but rather for something even earlier, the cultural wrong turn that led to Moody's status as one of the anointed ones of his— okay, *our*—generation. For me, that wrong turn starts around the time Stephen Dedalus goes to university in *A Portrait of the Artist as a Young Man* and echoes all the way through Don DeLillo's ponderously self-important rendering of Bobby Thomson's shot heard round the world in the opening chapter of *Underworld.* What I'm trying to say is that Moody's badness is a little less inexplicable if you look at him as the lowest common denominator of a generation of writers *and readers* who have long since forgotten what the modernist and postmodernist assaults on linearity were actually about, and as such have lost the ability to tell the difference between ambiguity and inscrutability, ambition and bombast, of writers who are taken at face value when they're being ironic and deemed ironic when they're telling it straight—assuming, that is, they know the difference themselves. Assuming, I should add, they actually *have* a subject.

"What we are getting today," B.R. Myers wrote in the summer of 2001, in a refreshingly dissenting article about contemporary literature in *The Atlantic Monthly*, "is a remarkably crude form of affectation: a prose so repetitive, so elementary in its syntax, and so numbing in its overuse of wordplay that it often demands less concentration than the average 'genre' novel." Myers goes on: "Today's Serious Writers fail even on their own postmodern terms. They urge us to move beyond our old-fashioned preoccupation with content and plot, to focus on form instead—and then they subject us to the least-expressive form, the least-expressive *sentences*, in the history of the American novel." Among the younger generation of writers, I can think of no author who indulges more in this "remarkably crude form of affectation" than Moody, who once described his style as "a more natural albeit slightly more hysterical kind of line length." "Line length," of course, refers to poetry, not prose, but the imprecision is typical of Moody's half-thought-out rhetoric: the buzzwords here are "natural" and "hysterical," the rest approximations, filler. "I just hit it," he went on. "I just landed the vein in a way. And I suddenly realized that it was okay for me to write these long, torrid sentences and that people would still read the work and many people would be really excited by it." The segue is revealing: Moody's criteria for his linguistic style is not that it be coherent but that it be "okay," that "people would still read the work" and "be really excited by it." As with the books themselves, what comes through here is Moody's urgent, indeed "hysterical" desire to be heard, and, in its defense, Moody's audience is surely not the first to be "excited" by the sweat stains under a preacher's arms rather than the "torrid sentences" of the book he holds in his hands.

Let us take, by way of example, the opening paragraph of *The Black Veil.*

So there's the matter of our crimes. The remembrance of our misdoings is grievous to us; the burden of them is intolerable. Lies, whispered, of friends' indiscretions; instances of envy—when we hate the people we love; peccadilloes, filched office supplies; inflated expense accounts; violent obsessions of all kinds, reckless speeding, a fender bender whose scene we left; the belt from Macy's we slipped into our own belt loops (they're the easiest thing to take); a copy of Montaigne, nineteenth century edition, never returned to the library; a kiss stolen from someone else's lover; a night out of state upon a tanned mattress when the energy of adultery seemed so persuasive that we concealed from ourselves all memory of our spouses; gifts never sent; allegiances never acknowledged; inexplicable cruelties to people with bad luck; inexplicable cruelties to friends; a waiter we upbraided that time; we cheated at cards; we cheated at tennis; we cheated at backgammon or at chess or at some board game of our childhood; we tripped that guy in the backfield and then waltzed in for the goal; we took things for granted, took privileges for rights; we demanded things in no way due us. And then with some of us there are worse crimes, crimes unspeakable, though we might write of them, like robbery, battery, or rape. We fell into coercion or abuse or full-scale embezzlement or even murder, the murder of innocents perhaps; we committed crimes of rage so that afterwards we couldn't sleep, couldn't forget, couldn't think straight, and whispered to ourselves, revisiting these instances of our transgression. There's the matter of our crimes.

Readers familiar with Moody's work will recognize in this paragraph the incantatory declarations with which he has begun all his books since *The Ice Storm.* These openings are less set-up to what follows than contest of wills between Moody and his reader, a calculated assault by the former on the aesthetic proprieties of the latter. *The Ice Storm* declares its grandness of intent in the hyperbole of subject matter (all of Nixonian America) whereas *Purple America* is more gestural, opening with a two- or three-thousand-word sentence riffing on John 11:26 (whosoever liveth and believeth in me shall never die). In fact, these beginnings are nothing more than transparent attempts at linguistic virtuosity: the former is just a list, the latter a series of sentences faintly echoing biblical rhythms and linked by commas rather than periods. But mostly they're superfluous, which is what, finally, makes them so annoying. Moody starts his books like a boxer talking trash before the bout, as if trying to make his opponent forget that the only thing that really matters is how hard and how well you throw your fists after the bell rings. But in reality the clash between Moody and reader is less pugilistic than pissing contest, particularly if that reader happens to be a man; and if that reader happens to be a writer then the experience becomes even more inflammatory. For me, the beginning of a Rick Moody book is a bit like having a stranger walk up and smack me in the face, and then stand there waiting to see if I'm man enough to separate him from his balls.

But not even I was prepared for the arcana which opens *The Black Veil.* I have been staring at these 270 words for three or four months now, and I still find myself unable to reason them out. Every connection I try to make leads to new disjunctions. There is the stagy and false informality of that leading "So," the conjugal insinuation of "our," the odd choice of "misdoings" rather than "misdeeds." Why? And what is that dash doing between "envy" and "when"? Though the antecedent of that parenthetical "they're" is obviously "belt," the plural leads one to think it refers to "belt loops," giving rise to an image of the author sawing off the belt loops of department-store pants; or, similarly, the indefinite "a waiter" followed by the definite "that time": is he remembering a specific occasion, or is he not? And what exactly is a "tanned mattress"? This isn't poetic license we're talking about here, it's basic Freshman Comp. stuff—it's just wrong, grammatically, stylistically, and, most importantly, semantically. *It just doesn't make sense.* I mean, wasn't there a single person to point out that "the murder of innocents" is a redundancy on a par with "wet water"? That what this passage cries out for is in fact "matter"? Not simply the names of crimes but their substance: details, concrete information. That, for example, describing a volume of Montaigne as a "nineteenth century edition" is less a telling detail than a grab at the authority that attaches to canonical figures (in this case the very man who invented the term "essai")? Wouldn't Moody's purposes be better served if readers knew whether the stolen edition came in one or more volumes? If it was one hundred years old, or two, or somewhere in between? If it was Florio's 1603 translation, which is practically a foreign language itself, or Hazlitt's more modern 1856 edition, or if Moody read it in French? *Que sait-tu?* one wants to say to the writer: What do you *know?*

Possibly the only real accomplishment of this paragraph is Moody's insinuation of a bond between himself and the reader.

His "we" invokes a collective self, as though to suggest at the outset that this "memoir" is not just about Rick Moody and not just about the reader, but about the larger society "we" are both a part of. Your inclusion in Moody's "we"—in effect, your guilt—begins the moment you begin reading *The Black Veil*, and even if *you* aren't guilty of "crimes unspeakable" some other member of the nebulous "we" you've become a part of is, and as such you share in his or her responsibility and blame. Or at least that's my take on it. No real characters emerge in the 300 pages which follow this paragraph; rather, they're filled by Moody's singular-yet-shared consciousness, half object, half subject, like the shadow of a finger in front of a camera lens. There *is* a more-or-less straightforward narrative—two actually, the story of Moody's depression, addiction, and recovery; and a genealogical investigation of the Moody family's long and singularly undramatic tenure in New England—but these two stories proceed less by scenes than by riffs, stale tableaux which could probably be broken down into, say, twelve steps or so, but which are mainly there to set the stage for pages upon pages of banal yet apparently heartfelt hyperbole. Still, as near as I can parse it, the underlying premise of this book—the reason why we're muddling through such I'm-being-ironic-or-am-I? questions as "How many pages can you read of the very philosophy from which you, contemporary American, emerged, before you yawn and reach for the antithetical comforts, for the remote-control, for the beer in its Styrofoam sleeve, for the joint that goes around?"—is that Moody, who suffered from clinical depression and alcoholism into his twenties (he's sober now, fortysomething, and, apparently, well-adjusted), came to see his condition as nothing less than the "genetic" "inheritance" of his patrilineal line, in particular one Joseph "Handkerchief" Moody, a late-eighteenth-century New England minister who might—although he might not—have been the inspiration for Nathaniel Hawthorne's short story "The Minister's Black Veil."

Now, this story, and his ancestral link to it, seem particularly important to Moody. Chapter Three is devoted to a Lit. Crit. 101 reading of the text, quotations from which appear regularly throughout his memoir, and the story in its entirety shows up as an appendix, a borrowing almost but not quite as pretentious as Jeanette Winterson's use of a dozen pages from the score of Strauss' *Der Rosenkavalier* as a coda to her novel *Art and Lies*. In a prefatory footnote to his story, Hawthorne mentions that Handkerchief Moody "made himself remarkable by the same eccentricity that is here related." That is, he wore a veil in daily life. "In [Handkerchief Moody's] case, however, the symbol has a different import. In early life he had accidentally killed a beloved friend; and from that day till the hour of his own death, he hid his face from men." In Hawthorne's story, Parson Hooper's reason for donning the veil is never revealed, and it is the subject of much speculation among his fellow villagers; Moody, ignoring Hawthorne's admonition that "the symbol has a different import," reads the veil as an indication of a crime Hooper is concealing, a crime he shares with his fellow Puritans, both fictional and real—i.e., with Handkerchief Moody, our present-day Moody, and "you, contemporary American," since in Moody's conception all of contemporary America "emerged" from "the very philosophy" of the Puritans. The connection, "genetic," "symbolic," or otherwise, between Rick and Handkerchief Moody's morbidity strikes me as tenu-

ous at best—especially after you find out they're probably not
even related—but the gist of the idea seems to be that Moody's
depression was a scrim that simultaneously concealed and
pointed up some secret sin committed by not just him and not
just Handkerchief Moody and the other males in his family
line, but by, in ever-widening circles of implication, all Americans, contemporary or otherwise, and if I follow his reasoning,
which can be difficult since it proceeds primarily by rhythm
and evocation rather than logic, then this book is meant to tell
us what that sin is. By the time I finished reading, I was convinced the book *was* the sin.

"To be an American," Moody writes in one of the few syntactically lucid sentences in the book (unfortunately it's also
the third to last), "to be a citizen of the West, is to be a murderer." The syntax is clear, the semantics less so. Moody's
American murderers seem to be guilty of the crimes that have
obsessed the politically correct for the past couple of decades:
the assumption of heterosexual privilege (at the depth of his
depression Moody's constant fear was that he *"was going to be
raped"*), the innate violence of masculinity ("I think of all *dead
girls* expunged by philosophies and theologies of the mascu-
line"), and of course the theft of this continent from the Indians
("the black scar of Manifest Destiny, the recollection of which
should cause aggravated insomnia in all North American
adults"). Although it's sort of refreshing to see a straight white
male taking a hard p.c. line, Moody's absolutist construction
("to be an American," "to be a citizen of the West," "to be a murderer": this young man has none of Hamlet's doubt) betrays an
unacknowledged and contradictory division. For example: "the
brutality visited upon those who preceded us here" is what

Moody writes in ostensible reference to the invasion of the Americas by Europe. But both "those" and "us" lack clear antecedents, and as such the latter hearkens all the way back to the "us" 's and "we" 's and "our" 's of *The Black Veil*'s opening incantation. "We," it would seem, are not merely Americans, we are also straight and white and male, since these are the attributes of power and thus of victimizing; our victims—"those" who are not "us," who are not straight and white and male— are therefore not American. They make up a separate nation.

This is all fun for me, but I do want to be clear about one thing: I don't think Moody's racist, sexist, or homophobic. I just think he's a bad writer. But that has consequences. *The Black Veil* isn't simply a bad idea badly rendered. It's so bad that it's easy to see it as in league with the very crimes it seeks to redress. Here, as in the books which preceded it, the language Moody employs is so fundamentally imprecise that it can't help but tell untruths. There is the innocuous generality: "First, the guest room, with the orderly neglect of all guest rooms" (*The Ice Storm*). There is the denigration of the physical world in favor of a fancy conceit: "Rail lines marked the perimeters of Haledon, this isosceles triangle in the flat Eastern part of the Garden State. Freight trains ran through it like blood cells, carrying unpronounceable compounds and toxins. They rumbled past the accidents at crossing gates, past the crime scenes and late-night waste burials" (*Garden State*). The metaphor works fine here: what doesn't work is the description. At the end of the passage our only image of Haledon, New Jersey—of the "accidents" and "crime scenes" and "waste burials"—remains an outline, unfilled by the metaphor it contains. There is a certain poignancy to these stereotypical generalities and slipshod metaphors. They speak of the difficulty of individual expression, of the homogenization and simplification of life by the very tools which seek to understand its complexity. But they lack depth: Moody's meta-descriptions never show individuality in the process of being squashed—or, for that matter, of finding a way to express itself—and this, besides being dramatically uninteresting, is not an accurate reflection of the world he's describing. The war may indeed be lost, but that doesn't mean the battle's over, that individual soldiers don't continue to fight and lose (and fight and win) the occasional skirmish.

And then there's this:

> Jen packed up for her rehabilitation center, in Armonk, which had a pastoral name. Tired of being henpecked by her aunts, I thought; grief-stricken about her mother, desiring of good relations with the remaining women of her tribe. The last weeks before her leaving were such a wreck that I thought, in a spate of intuitive reasoning, that it was a *good* to get her out of the house, because she was getting *really bad*, and I didn't want her looking at me in my disgrace, and all we did was sleep and drink, so it was fine. She got in the car with the rebuilt front end, packed up some practical outfits, took off. I misunderstood what a precarious moment it was, as Handkerchief Moody must have felt calling for a midwife on the eve of the birth of his daughter Lucy. Once Jen was out of the house, I slumped further into the cave-dwelling part of my back brain. The lonely villain in a monster movie, a suzerain of reclusion, drinking, loathing myself, going out and feeling afraid, cynical, contemptuous, literally disgusted by *my own shadow*, by everything that had to do with me, by my borders and everything contained

within my borders, the trouble I had wrought, everything I'd gotten into, while the streets around me were *full of riots of sexual assault*, women of leisure and men of leisure and men of leisure dressed as women, underneath the punctilious exterior of the society in which I had been raised, libertine cravings, the unquenchable urges toward excess of carnal delight, everywhere bawds and adulterers, pedophiles and bestialists, lovers of incest and masochism, all institutions of the civilized America were window-dressing for the excursion of sexual power into the ghetto of the powerless, a sequence of rapes, Manifest Destiny as the rationalization of genocide by method of rape, the Republican Party as rationalization of genocide, Fundamentalist Christianity as rationalization of genocide, every kind word uttered to another libertine was the means by which sodomy would be exercised. . . .

Here, as in his memoir's opening paragraph—as in virtually every paragraph of this book—is patently specious psychological and symbolic amplification of a kind I haven't seen since the last time I dipped into some of Freud's wackier case studies. But even Freud was willing to admit that sometimes a cigar is just a cigar: Moody's free-associative mind—elsewhere he makes reference to a "virus of language," which seems particularly useful as a description of his own sentence style—simply cannot let things be what they are. There are any number of problems with this book, but in the end it always comes back to the prose. A writer's words, more than his narratives, characters, and themes, are the closest we have to a blueprint of his vision, and in Rick Moody's words there is a single striking consistency. You could call it an ever-widening gap between signifier and signified, or you could call it lies. Or you could just call it what it is, which is bullshit.

And yet.

There is that urgency I mentioned before, the hysterical desire to be heard. For all its shrillness, Moody's volume strikes me as something more than the antics of a child needing attention. I say this as a fellow novelist: though he's never put together a single sentence I would call indispensable, there *is* a true empathetic undercurrent in Moody's work. I find the same current in the work of David Foster Wallace and Jeffrey Eugenides and Colson Whitehead but not in the work of Richard Powers and Dave Eggers and Donald Antrim and Jonathan Franzen and Lethem, find it also in the work of Thomas Pynchon but not Don DeLillo, here and there in Barth and Barthelme but almost entirely absent in Fowles and Hawkes and Gaddis, in *Lolita* but not *Pale Fire*—in, that is to say, the early Joyce (the first one and a half fictions) but not in the last two and a half.

What I am talking about here is the most esoteric strain of twentieth-century literature, what some people think of as the highest of high canonical postmodernism, and what I, with all due respect to Colson Whitehead, prefer to think of as the white man's ivory tower. My friend and fellow novelist Jim Lewis (he shows up in *The Black Veil* under the pseudonym "Irv") prefers the term Geek Lit, but I think that a venereal designation is unavoidable in discussing literature's secret society, the Skull and Bones of the novelist's set. These boys have their own little club going, and like all clubs it's defined as much by its gate-crashers as its blueblood members. Again, this isn't meant to malign the aforementioned writers. I don't want to suggest that they're uniformly talentless or misguided, or that there's a conspiracy among them, or between them and the editors of the *New Yorker* or *Harper's* or the *Paris Review;* or that they invest any of their energy in excluding others from the upper echelons of the literary world. All I'm suggesting is that these writers (and their editors) see themselves as the heirs to a bankrupt tradition. A tradition that began with the diarrheic flow of words that is *Ulysses,* continued on through the incomprehensible ramblings of late Faulkner and the sterile inventions of late Nabokov (two writers who more or less sold out their own early brilliance), and then burst into full, foul life in the ridiculous dithering of John Barth and John Hawkes and William Gaddis, the reductive cardboard constructions of Donald Barthelme, the word-by-word wasting of a talent as formidable as Thomas Pynchon's, and finally broke apart like a cracked sidewalk beneath the weight of the stupid—just plain stupid—tomes of Don DeLillo. This is a tradition that has systematically divested itself of any ability to comment on anything other than its own inability to comment on anything, a malaise that only David Foster Wallace has the good sense to lament. A tradition which has turned the construction of a novel into a formal exercise, judged either by the inexpressive or inscrutable floribundity of its prose (Eggers, Wallace, and Moody) or the lifeless carpentry of its parts (Antrim, Eugenides, Franzen, Lethem, Powers, and Whitehead), rather than by the quasi-mystical animating aspect of literature that even a rational Englishman like E.M. Forster called "prophecy." And that's a shame, because I think Rick Moody, alone among his self-selecting generation, has something to say and the means with which to say it. Something which might actually meet Forster's criterion if it were developed in an artful, thoughtful manner:

Rick Moody is sad.

I can think of no more relevant reason to write books today than out of an overwhelming sense of despair at the state of the world—it is in fact why I spend so much time writing book reviews. When I wrote my last review anthrax was traveling through the U.S. Postal Service and smart bombs were decimating Afghanistan; now we're waiting to find out if Pakistan and India are going to fight the first-ever tactical nuclear war. Global warming, overpopulation, the worldwide AIDS epidemic, the ever-increasing distance between supposedly democratic governments and their electorates, the decimation of culture after culture by the relentless spread of the Disneyfied kitsch of the American entertainment complex, and the incredibly sad, horrible, hopelessness-inducing fact that people still can't say what they really mean to one another after seven or so millennia of human civilization: life really, really sucks right now. I'm not claiming things are any worse than they've ever been, merely that there's just cause for sadness, and no writer strikes me as more despondent about the state of the world than Rick Moody. That he hides his despondency behind literary bravura and posturing is itself a cause for sadness; but I still believe Moody could write well if he wanted to. He has a true writer's sensibility. His stories have the heft and shape of cultural narratives. There was even a moment at the end of *The Ice Storm* when my heart went out to him. The utter sorrow that infused every word was real ("His cry emerged, long and hoarse and elastic and then muted, choked off"), even as it seemed independent of the simple story it told and the sugar-coated moral it poured on top ("Elena knew that apology was the impossible paragraph, its words were like the secret names of God"). That sadness is oddly muted in *The Black Veil.* One feels less connection to the writer as he details his real neurosis than when he's detailing the tribulations of his fictional Hood family. In part that distancing is a result of Moody's ever-deteriorating prose, in part his unwillingness to own his feelings, preferring instead to blame someone else—his ancestors, society, or, my theory, metaphor. Moody's virus is not so much of language as of language's need to resort to comparison in order to represent intangible things like thoughts, emotions, the divine. Though he pretends that these comparisons bring him closer to what he's trying to describe, something—his pen, or his subconscious—knows that in fact he's wandering farther and farther from the truth, which is why the Rick Moody conjured in the pages of *The Black Veil* feels even more artificial than the people who inhabit his fiction. Talk about *weltschmerz.*

Rick Moody, his very own creation, his very own exemplary American, cannot lift his own veil of projection and see that, indeed, Parson Hooper's veil "has a different import" than the one worn by Handkerchief Moody. Hawthorne specifically says the veil is *not* a symbol of a crime, a fact which Moody ignores, and in doing so ignores the fact that Hawthorne was interested in man's nature rather than his actions, a narrative chain of cause and effect based not on an individual's history but the history of the species. In a post-Freudian age, it is understandable that we should interpret Hawthorne's fascination with external markings—the black veil, the scarlet letter, the birthmark—in a psychological context, but that's anachronistic and simplistic. The notion that human beings commit crimes isn't exactly interesting, let alone revelatory; about the only thing that Moody's belief that people ought to wear their guilt like a caul tells us is that he has not, in fact, escaped the legacy of his ancestors, genetic or otherwise. Ultimately, *The Black Veil* is less an explication of an American crime or American guilt (of either the criminal or psychological variety) than of a particular American need to assign blame or refuse it. Rick Moody is a Puritan, his memoir nothing more than a witch hunt. But his culprit, he would see if he pulled the wool from his own eyes, is himself.

And now I'll tell you *my* truth: I went into this review thinking Moody was a faker, a poser. Shooting him off his plinth, I thought, would be easier than shooting fish in a barrel. But whatever else he is, he's the genuine article. A writer of one terrible book after another, but a writer nonetheless. If you want to know the difference between a real writer and all those wanna-bes who punish us with their memoirs and literary novels, it's this: the real writer is incapable of seeing the world through anything but the prism of metaphor and narrative, which renders that world as falsely as chronology renders the progress of time. The real writer suspects that character is just a byproduct of these two forces—that what we think of as ourselves is nothing more than an assortment of chemicals acted upon by internal and external stimuli—and in some ways it's his urgent need to disprove this hypothesis, to assert at least the possibility of an existence independent of fate, that drives him to write fiction. It's true, it's true, what you've always suspected is true: it's ourselves we blame, ourselves we're trying to save. Not you.

All of which is possibly just the essay-length way of saying that I hate Rick Moody's books, but there's always a moment in each one of them when I get mad at myself for hating them.

But then, alas, the moment passes.

11

Kurt's Conundrum

Timequake by Kurt Vonnegut

T*imequake*, Kurt Vonnegut's latest book, and, according to the author, his last, is virtually impossible to appreciate without an extensive knowledge of his previous work. As far as I can tell this is intentional, and it could be considered a flaw or a virtue depending on one's view of literature in general and Kurt Vonnegut in particular, but at the end of the day one thing remains: if you're not familiar with the characters who have populated Vonnegut's writing since, say, 1965—including Vonnegut himself, and his fictional alter-ego Kilgore Trout—then *Timequake* will come across as nothing more than what it is, namely, a few salvaged fragments from an abandoned fiction project glued together with autobiographical sketches and aphorisms. *Timequake One*, as Vonnegut refers to the original book, seems to have started out as just another Vonnegut novel, but *Timequake Two*, as he calls the finished product, has been reconceived as the legend to the Vonnegut map, less a final act than a curtain call, a thin rubber band holding together the braided but still distinct strands of a forty-five-year career and a seventy-five-year life.

IN A PAIR OF ARTICLES that appeared on the front page of the *New York Observer* in October 1997, headlined "Twilight of the Great Literary Beasts," Sven Birkerts and David Foster Wallace lament the decline in quality of the work produced by America's greatest living straight white male novelists (it is not for us to ask why). They name as these authors Saul Bellow, Norman Mailer, Philip Roth, and John Updike. Neither mentions Kurt Vonnegut, even though Wallace goes so far as to name the trio of Roth, Mailer, and Updike "the great narcissists," a title to which Vonnegut has a far more legitimate claim. At any rate, Bellow and the narcissists have a host of prizes between them which Vonnegut certainly *can't* claim—a Nobel, and a trophy case full of National Book Awards and Pulitzers—but Vonnegut has one thing they never will, which is a cult following. Vonnegut is not in fact a patriarch of the extended family of American writers; he is instead its crazy uncle, the old codger full of wit and wisdom and more than a little bullshit. Take, for example, the prologue to *Timequake:* "I have pretended in this book I will still be alive for the clambake in 2001. In chapter 46, I imagine myself as still alive in 2010. Sometimes I say I'm in 1996, where I really am, and sometimes I say I am in the midst of a rerun following a timequake, without making clear distinctions between the two situations. I must be nuts." Forget that last sentence: that's just Vonnegut trying to throw us off the trail. The key word here is *pretend*. Pretending is something children do—writers *create*, or *invent*, or *foment*; at the very least, as Vonnegut does in his second sentence, they *imagine*. Vonnegut's use of a child's term is characteristic of the regressive urge that informs all his work, but it is, more importantly, a pointed reference to the infantilized position he finds himself in as the titular object of worship of the Cult of Vonnegut.

Anyone with a little gray hair can play the crazy uncle, but cult status is something that can only be bestowed: it can't be claimed. But, for the same reason, it's also a state one can sink below but never rise above. It is, in other words, a trap. In Vonnegut's case, it's a very lucrative trap. He's sold millions of books, but what he's been denied is legitimacy, or, more to the point, influence. Cult writers almost always have a political or social or aesthetic agenda—said agenda being what keeps them out of the mainstream—and Vonnegut's pet peeves certainly aren't hard to find. He's railed against violence in general and war in particular, against the way technology is reducing the ability of human beings to find meaningful work, against our treatment of the young, the elderly, the poor, and the otherwise "useless" members of society, against greed, against television, against semicolons (he says they don't mean anything), and against the lionizing of literary figures—both writers and their creations. Fans and critics have long noted his opinions, even praised him for them (praise which seems always to include the phrase "Vintage Vonnegut!"), and ignored him. Vonnegut has been trapped in this Cassandra role for nearly thirty years—not Cassandra, really, but something even worse. It's not that Vonnegut's fans don't believe what he has to say. They just don't seem to care.

But perhaps, in Vonnegut's case, that's to be expected. Another of the distinguishing characteristics of cult writers is monomania. Charles Bukowski's was sex and drugs, Hunter S. Thompson's is drugs and sex, but Kurt Vonnegut's obsession, the single theme which has dominated every one of his books from *Player Piano* in 1952 to *Timequake* today, is the futility of human action, so it's hardly surprising that his followers have chosen not to act on his words of wisdom. *Followers* doesn't seem too strong a word, for Vonnegut's stories have always read like religious parables. The prototypical Vonnegut hero, from Malachi Constant to Eliot Rosewater to Dwayne Hoover to Rudy Waltz, attempts to achieve the serenity of the Buddha while facing the torments that beset Christ. He is, in other words, a eunuch and a cog on the wheel of fate, and the only thing that distinguishes tragedy from comedy is whether the hero learns to accept his powerlessness. The truly tragic heroes are the ones who don't, but there have been fewer and fewer tragic heroes in the recent Vonnegut novels. Rather, they rush headlong into oblivion, into unknowing, or, more simply, into death.

Maybe that's why Vonnegut has always struck me as the real tragic figure of his stories: he himself seems not to have given up, else why continue to write? Though he was raised and remains an atheist, he is one of those atheists who longs for the simplicity of belief. In *Timequake* he writes of a friend's loss of faith in Catholicism, "I thought that was too much to lose"; he also reports, tellingly, that one of the few literary quotations which still obsesses him is Christ's remark "Who is it they say I am?" Maybe I'm just romanticizing him now—but then, that's another characteristic of cult writers, isn't it? Writers who are merely great—writers such as Mailer and Bellow and

Roth and Updike—write stories which become part of our dreams, but cult writers are themselves dreamed about. I would like to think that some writers could actually be both, and I would suggest Vonnegut is the most likely candidate for that position, but it has not yet happened, and I wonder if this has something to do with the fact that he is still alive. Perhaps, as he insists repeatedly in *Timequake*, things will be better when he's dead; perhaps his followers will stop searching his books for some clue as to how their guru lives, and simply *read* them. But he seems to doubt it.

VONNEGUT HAS, in fact, tried to provide those clues. In his introduction to 1981's *Palm Sunday*, he kidded readers that his most recent effort is

> a marvelous new literary form. This book combines the tidal power of a major novel with the bone-rattling immediacy of front-line journalism—which is old stuff now, God knows, God knows. But I have also intertwined the flashy enthusiasms of musical theater, the lethal left jab of the short story, the sachet of personal letters, the oompah of American history, and oratory in the bow-wow style.

In fact *Palm Sunday* is nothing more or less than an autobiographical collage, at once a dressed-up collection of ephemera and a fiery, funny polemic from a writer on the threshold of old age. A single continuous narrative—the story of Vonnegut's life—proceeds via a series of detours: book reviews, commencement speeches, letters private and public, and a few borrowed texts.

What emerges, especially of Vonnegut's early years, is at once evocative and blandly general: there is the happiness of an "Edwardian" childhood lived in pre-Depression splendor in Indianapolis, Indiana (1922–29), the sudden descent into genteel squalor following the crash (1929–40), a couple of tries at college (1940–43, first at Cornell, then at the Carnegie Institute of Technology), and a stint in the U.S. Infantry which culminated in his capture in the Battle of the Bulge (1943–45). Then, in a period of less than two years, Vonnegut witnessed and miraculously survived the firebombing of Dresden as a POW, learned of his mother's suicide, saw the end of World War II, reentered university, and married for the first time. Five years later, after working as a reporter in Chicago and a p.r. man in Schenectady, New York, Vonnegut published his first short story at the age of twenty-eight; he abandoned public relations to write fiction on a freelance basis—those were the happy days before television, he reminds us, when a writer could support himself and his family just by writing short stories—and two years later, in 1952, he published his first novel, *Player Piano.*

Vonnegut published ten more books by the time he produced *Palm Sunday,* and as a result his readers were already familiar with these biographical details. Not that Vonnegut had indulged in autofiction; rather, he'd taken up the habit of including short prefaces to his novels. These prefaces, generally as unadorned as the novels which followed them were fantastic, provided brief bulletins on Vonnegut's life, and, as well, suggested certain real-world antecedents to the fictions they preceded. In fact, the evolution of these prefaces is as important as the novels themselves. The first appeared, appropriately enough, in Vonnegut's collection of short stories, *Welcome to the Monkey House*. In his next book, the preface had grown noticeably longer, and was simply labeled "chapter one." That book was 1969's *Slaughterhouse-Five*, the most autobiographical of Vonnegut's novels—Vonnegut uses the first chapter to demarcate what's made up from what's real—and it was also the novel which made his reputation, and began in earnest the Cult of Vonnegut. It shouldn't have been surprising then, when Vonnegut, flush with his first real success in two decades of writing, and also wary of that success, simply moved himself into the storyline of his next novel, *Breakfast of Champions*. But whether or not critics were surprised, they were certainly outraged, and thereafter Vonnegut moved out of his stories and back to his prefaces. The move could be seen as conciliatory, but Vonnegut is cleverer than that; despite the diminutizing label "preface" or "prologue," these notes are integral to the reading of his novels. Their primary purpose, and, as well, the purpose of *Palm Sunday*—in essence, an entire book of prefaces and prologues and author's notes—is to nip the growing Cult of Vonnegut in the bud. But despite his efforts to clear up the relationship between his art and his life, to expose himself as shyster, not shaman, as a simple storyteller rather than a maker of fables, the reverent adulation with which he and his books were greeted only continued to grow.

And so, by the time Vonnegut published *Palm Sunday* in 1981, he had been elected a member of the National Institute of Arts and Letters and received several honorary degrees (including one from the University of Chicago, which had unanimously rejected the Master's Thesis he submitted in 1947)—

and his primary audience had become high school students. *Palm Sunday* depicts a writer whose books are burned by schools (is it any wonder kids wanted to read them?) and who is invited to speak at fund-raisers for the American Civil Liberties Union, a writer privileged to provide introductions to books by Céline as well as Bob Elliot and Ray Goulding (famous comedians of his youth), but who wrote of *Slaughterhouse-Five:* "The Dresden atrocity, tremendously expensive and meticulously planned, was so meaningless, finally, that only one person on the entire planet got any benefit from it. I am that person. . . . One way or another, I got two or three dollars for every person killed. Some business I'm in." What emerges in *Palm Sunday* is the same struggle Vonnegut-as-character put before Kilgore Trout in *Breakfast of Champions*, and which Vonnegut-as-author puts before him one last time in *Timequake*, and that is the struggle, for an artist, between celebrity and anonymity, between vanity and purity, between, in the most loaded senses of the words, enthrallment and freedom. In *Palm Sunday* Vonnegut seems to think that it is still a choice, and at the book's close he coyly says, "I thank you for your sweetly faked attention." In *Timequake* he is deliberately more juvenile, more bitter, and more to the point: for some writers, the choice isn't theirs to make. "[I] never asked to be born in the first place" is how he puts it, and it seems clear he is referring not only to himself, but to the figure his followers have made of him.

It was only when I reread *Palm Sunday* that I finally understood why Vonnegut's attempts to demystify himself, and so defuse his cult, failed so miserably. With all his fastidious charting of the details of his professional life, fleshed out by nothing more than the tiniest snippets of autobiography, Vonnegut seemed to be creating a smokescreen, a smokescreen that engulfed both reader *and* writer. Thus, the personal details which could be glimpsed became less interesting than the things which we assumed Vonnegut was hiding. In book after book, Vonnegut told his readers precisely what his writing meant to him, but what he never said was why he wrote, and it was the thing not said, the *why* rather than the *what*, which became of paramount importance. It is only now, sixteen years after *Palm Sunday*, that we at last learn the truth: Vonnegut wasn't holding anything back. His is a life clearly divided in two—before he started writing, and after—and what came after clearly *is* his life. The *why*, in other words, is also the *what*, which is perhaps what he was trying to tell us all along. From *Palm Sunday:*

> So here I sit on the fourth floor of a town house on the East Side of New York City, the Capital of the World, with a report card on the past thirty years of my life—signed by myself and tacked to the wall. I look at all those grades, some high, some low, and I think that I am like the compulsive gambler who borrowed so much money from me and who could not pay me back: *I could not help myself* [my italics].

I'm going to stop there, not because I want to, but because I must—because it seems to me pointless to begin the otherwise joyous task of unboxing and assembling the vast puzzle of narrative and meaning Kurt Vonnegut has created in nineteen books. How many times does Vonnegut visit the planet Trafalmadore (three, I think)? How many books feature the made-up towns of Ilium, New York (again, three), and Midland City,

Ohio (six at last count)? Why are two different secretaries in two different novels named Francine Pefko (*Cat's Cradle* and *Breakfast of Champions*), and how is it that Kilgore Trout, according to *Timequake*, is still alive in 2001, when his tombstone in *Breakfast of Champions* says that he died in 1981? I leave these and a thousand more riddles to others, be they scholars or cultists, because, like Vonnegut, I cannot imagine the use in doing such things when I know that any attention I receive will be sweetly faked, and that ears will not prick up until I begin again to speculate on Vonnegut's life and motivations.

I will only say this: no writer I can think of has been more diligent nor more successful in *pretending*, despite what he describes as a limited cache of tools: "twenty-six phonetic symbols, ten numbers, and about eight punctuation marks." This disparagement of language aside, Vonnegut has proven endlessly, almost relentlessly creative in using it to tell new stories in new ways. Vonnegut was the first novelist to attempt to demystify the relationship between author and story within his text, to suggest that stories, be they children's cartoons or religious tracts, are nothing more than the product of individual imaginations and should be read as such, but this and all of his other formal innovations have gone unnoticed, lost somewhere between the glazed-eyed worship of his fans and the head-patting condescension of his critics ("Vintage Vonnegut!" indeed). And so, with each successive story, Vonnegut proved even more relentless in yoking his various inventions to that single theme of futility. His final novels, by which I mean the novels written since *Palm Sunday*, are as stylistically perfect as any written in the past twenty years, and they are also, for me, almost unbearable to read, because of the sense of hopeless-

ness—perhaps *helplessness* is a better word—which resonates
through every line.

And so, *Timequake.* Vonnegut named the literary form he
was creating in *Palm Sunday* a "blivet"—"two pounds of shit in
a one-pound bag"—but its codicil is something less than that,
something, really, like a trivet. Trivets are those little things
that protect your tabletop from the bottom of a hot serving
dish. I'm thinking here of the Midwestern variety, which in
contrast to the simplicity of their function tend to be ornate in
design and decoration, stiff wrought iron twisted into sinewy
roosters or weeping willows or old-fashioned smoke-spewing
locomotives. I call *Timequake* a trivet because its only real use is
to the cook and not to his diners—to Vonnegut rather than his
readers. Vonnegut's last book is less a piece of ephemera than
esoterica, and for that reason it is, more than any of the others,
the book he couldn't help himself from writing, and that his
readers won't help themselves from reading. And reading into.

12

Give Me Shelter:
In Praise of Rebecca Brown

Excerpts from a Family Medical Dictionary

I was seven years old when my father, hard on the heels of his failed third marriage, uprooted my sister and me and moved us from Long Island to Kansas. Tribune was a tiny town eighteen miles from the Colorado border, so named in honor of the great New York newspaperman. The admiration for him in the area is so great that the only other extant town in Greeley County is called Horace, and at one point there was a Hector as well, supposedly named after Greeley's dog. For a while I thought Horace Greeley had passed through following his famous admonition to go west, but now I suspect that's just local myth. Whatever the inspiration, the slightly absurd nature of the homage goes a long way toward explaining a homesteading relationship to the larger world—as if "Horace" and "Hector" and "Greeley" and "Tribune" could tack the county to the growing nation in its push from east to west. For a while, too, I thought my own family would push on,

that eventually we would abandon this dusty outpost strag-
gling along the skull- and snakeskin-lined dry bed of the
White Woman Creek. To me, Tribune was a point on a journey that would take us ever farther from Bay Shore—from
the ocean, my mother, my aunts and uncles and cousins,
and everything else that I had, until that point, considered
home.

I used to say I became a writer because we moved to Tribune. Now I think the story's a little different: I became a
writer because we did, in fact, move away. A year after we arrived, my father had not only finished plumbing the thirty-
two-bed Greeley County hospital, he'd also spent several
months recuperating from hepatitis in the new facility. Like the
good Code Hero he was, he fell in love with one of his nurses,
and a year later the five of us (my new stepmother had a daughter of her own) moved 225 miles across the state to Hutchinson. Hutch looked a lot more like Bay Shore than it did
Tribune. It had a population of about 35,000 to Tribune's eight
or nine hundred and, like Bay Shore, its residential streets were
laid out in a grid periodically intersected by major highways.
Its houses were varied in size and style, its yards shaded by
trees that didn't look as though they were dying of thirst. But
all this was less important than the simple fact that Hutchinson
was, like Bay Shore, bigger than my nine-year-old mind could
comprehend, whereas Tribune, even when we lived there,
seemed small enough to fit in my back pocket. Perhaps this is
the difference between a town and a city: a town ends. You can
walk down one street or another to a place where the houses
stop, duck between the second and third strands of a barbed-
wire fence, and find yourself on the open prairie. In the years

after we left Tribune that prairie grew and grew in my imagination, until it came to seem as unfenced and vast as the entire
Mescalero Escarpment floating atop the Ogallala Aquifer—the
midcontinental plateau and the vast underground reservoir
over which the grasses and grains of the Great Plains ripple
like a thousand-mile-wide sheet of gold velvet. It's an image I
have felt the need to describe in words ever since I left it behind.

And yet, for all its vastness, the prairie's mnemonic
markers are tiny things: the feathered ends of waist-high grass,
a rusty knotted section of abandoned barbed-wire fence, the
zigzagging flight of a jackrabbit. It's almost thirty years since
I lived in Tribune, and my memories of the place have taken
on the peculiar quality of early childhood reminiscences:
physically, even viscerally immediate, yet also tinged by myth. I
remember the way the wind that constantly bit down on the
flat earth would disappear when I jumped into the White
Woman Creek's dry gully. I remember the stinging pain of
prickly-pear cactus needles piercing my tennis shoes; the
spine-tingling chill of a rattlesnake's warning when I crashed
through a tangle of juniper and tumbleweed; a cow's skeleton,
burnished white and stretched over a dozen feet where the
wind and coyotes had worried the last shreds of meat off the
bones. One time it rained and the desert flowers revealed their
pale pink and violet petals for a few hours. Another time it
didn't rain for so long that the ground lifted up and blew away
in a twenty-four-hour tidal wave of dust. The only time I ever
saw a tornado was in Tribune. Triangular and dark, it poked
from an elongated mass of dark cloud on the horizon like a
thorn from a tree branch—and seemed, at that distance, no   .

more threatening. And one time, I remember, I stumbled across a coyote den.

At first glance, the den looked like nothing more than a hole in the ground. In fact there were two: twinned entrances to a trough four or five feet long and covered in the center by a tiny bridge of earth no more than eighteen inches square. I'd've crawled through it if it had been big enough, but it wasn't even that big: the hollow of sheltered earth beneath the tunnel's strut was hardly bigger than a big mixing bowl. Grass still grew from the surface of the strut, wisps of root bristled its rounded underside. The grass at both entrances had at some point been worn away by the comings and goings of the band but the powdery soil was bare now, of tracks, bones, stray tufts of fur: whoever had sheltered there had abandoned the place long before I happened by. Indeed, there was so little to the den that it's hard, now, to find the words to describe it. And yet on the vast blank canvas of the open prairie it seemed hugely significant, an essential architecture that reminds me more than anything else of Tutankhamen's tomb. As my generation learned in grade school, King Tut's architects eschewed a monumental edifice for subterranean invisibility: no pyramid, just a hole in the ground. Their goal, we learned, was to safeguard their pharaoh's grave from thieves, but in the case of the den before me, the treasure that had been protected wasn't dead but alive. And thinking of that now, years later, it occurs to me that the den's purpose probably wasn't to protect its occupants from the elements—from nature—but rather from enemies. Plains coyotes have only the one predator, and on a flat horizon the only place to hide from him is underground.

I mention this coyote den because every time I try to sum up Rebecca Brown's writing it fills my mind, in lieu of some more literary or laudatory phrase. And I invest it with so much backstory because it seems, by itself, a mean illustration for a writer who's carved out one of the most distinct, powerful— and, alas, unread—oeuvres in contemporary American literature. The only shelter plainer than that coyote den would have been a hole in the ground, the kind a dog digs to cool off on hot days. But the architecture that informed the den's center strut set it apart from a purely minimal effort. It might have been instinct which caused the coyote to build in such a manner, but instinct doesn't preclude choice: on some primal level, the crude engineering that went into that minuscule arch marked a decision, away from self-denial, toward self-indulgence. As such it demarcated a line between poverty and luxury without really being either. Instead, by indicating that both worse and better states exist—states in which one is more or less comfortable, more or less safe—it marked the beginning of want.

It's this liminality that seems to me the heart of Rebecca Brown's project. The tininess of her books (not one is more than 200 pages), their cloistered mental environments and stripped-down prose, define an edge between starvation and subsistence, between not quite and just barely enough. On one side death, on the other decadence, in between a universe as taut as a tightrope—and every bit as important to the person depending upon it. The fact that coyotes take over other animals' abandoned dens as often as they dig their own only makes the image more fitting. Brown has been known to appropriate stories in the postmodern manner (in her 1984 debut collection, *The Evolution of Darkness*, the story "Annie" satirically reimagines Annie Oakley as a temporally displaced lesbian antihero, while *The Dogs*, a novel from 1998, contains several chapters that echo the accounts of Christian mystics in order to characterize a modern woman's inexplicable, terrifying visions) but it would be more accurate to say that Brown's books take up residence within certain tropes—of narrative, character, even information—expanding their narrow confines until she's created a space big enough to accommodate her needs. Brown has tapped into medieval history to show the effect of divorce on the feuding parties' progeny in the 1989 novel *The Children's Crusade*, and in *The Terrible Girls*, a series of linked stories from 1990, she glosses the kind of revolutionary zeal that informs Dostoevsky's *Demons* or Dickens' *A Tale of Two Cities*. Now, in *Excerpts From a Family Medical Dictionary*, Brown presents us with a slim memoir whose story—that of her mother's death from cancer—is organized around a series of definitions of medical terms: "anemia," "metastasis," "illusion," "unction," "remains."

True to its title, *Excerpts* elides everything extraneous to its deathbed vigil. There is no celebration of its protagonist's long prosperous life, no minimalizing of death's scope by placing it within some diminishing context. In *The Gifts of the Body*, a 1998 novel about a homecare worker who takes care of three PWAs, only one of the narrator's charges dies, an elderly woman whose final moments eerily prefigure those of Brown's mother. Though the novel proffers no illusions about the other characters' prognoses (the book was written just before protease inhibitors became available), the story allows its readers to "hope again" through the magic of truncation. Just as the novel offers no "before" to any of its characters' lives, it also frees them from an "after" which would almost certainly be death. By contrast, *Excerpts'* slice of time is cut from the very end of the loaf, the end of the line; the book's first words are, tellingly, "In memory of Barbara Ann Wildman Brown, 1928–1997," and in its opening chapter Barbara Brown is already exhibiting symptoms of the illness that will soon take her life. As a result of this extreme foreshortening, only slight traces of her character emerge, but what we do see evinces a Midwestern self-sufficiency that is by turns endearing and enduring. When chemotherapy makes her bleed "from her lips and gums and out of her ears," she doesn't complain but instead tries to rinse the blood from her pillowcase before anyone sees it. She neither laments the loss of her hair nor tries to smile it away; instead she orders several caps from a catalog and "hoped they would arrive before my brother did on his next visit. She said she didn't want to have to wear one of those old ski caps for him and she certainly didn't want him to see her bald." When the doctor tells her that the chemo isn't working—that, in other words, her death is upon her—"Chris told me that my mother's body had not shifted when the doctor told her this. She said my mother's body was not surprised." And when finally she has become so ill that Rebecca and her partner Chris and sister Betty have to bathe her in bed, "some of the time she looked at us but most of the time her eyes were away or closed."

But this isn't really a book about character, or even about narrative. It is only about death. There is no story to summarize—or, rather, the story is contained in the first paragraph, in every paragraph thereafter.

My mother started planning her trip in January. She was going to drive her new car from Silver City, the town she'd retired to two summers before, to my sister's in L.A. She'd do this on my sister's spring break and the two of them and my sister's son would drive together up the coast to see me and Chris. But that was the year of all that rain and some of the highways collapsed so my mother called in March and said they were going to postpone the trip.

Foreshadowing in elegies is like cigarette smoke in film noir: it's simply part of the package. But if *Excerpts* doesn't give in to the self-serving dictates of aesthetics or convention (and let's face it, cancer has become, in narrative terms, less a fatal disease than a gift, a learning experience, a personal triumph), it doesn't rail against them either. In true elegiac manner, nearly every word of *Excerpts* indicates the death to come. By the time we read the word "postpone" in the first paragraph—if not simply the word "started"—we know Barbara Brown's trip is never going to happen. Indeed, it takes a mere seventy pages for the first glimmer of disease ("She answered breezily that she'd caught the flu or something and hadn't quite shaken it yet") to progress to death ("Her face was yellow and waxy and smooth. Her cheeks were flat and her eyes were sunk and one of them was open. I tried to close it."). The entire book is only ninety-three pages long.

Though Brown the daughter tells her mother that "It's going to be ok" when the first tumor is found, Brown the writer never wavers in her focus. "I only see her start to die in retrospect," she writes. "In retrospect she dies over and over again." When I read those lines, I was reminded of

Wordsworth's famous dictum that "Poetry is the spontaneous overflow of powerful feelings; it takes its origin from emotion recollected in tranquility." The writing life has only a few curses, and this is perhaps the greatest: writers must continually revisit their most painful moments in order to make their work. As such, there is a dualism in *Excerpts* between daughter and writer, a subtly felt split which reaches its climax in the moments just after Barbara Brown dies. "I went to my mother's room and touched her, her face and her pulse, and I saw her face and I said to my sister and Chris, 'She's dead.' Chris touched my mother and said she was. She was dead." Look at all the doubles here: the touching of the face and then the looking at it, Rebecca's touch and then her partner Chris', the first "She's dead" and the confirmation: "She was dead." That first "She's dead" is almost a question, but the second, I realized, is not so much a confirmation as a depersonalization of what's happened. Chris' words indicate that Barbara Brown is not merely dead to her daughter, but to everyone else as well: to the people who inhabit the world she once lived in, and to the people who are reading about her death now. The first of each of these actions belongs to the daughter, but the second belongs to the writer, and thus to the reader. A personal loss becomes cultural, the complementary inverse of Donne's "any man's death diminishes me." Earlier in "Meditation #17," Donne writes, "The church is Catholic, universal, so are all her actions; all that she does belongs to all." Brown professes no church, no god—in some way, no theme even—but in offering her mother's death to readers in this way she still manages to convey that same sense of interconnectedness, of "all . . . all . . . all" that Donne felt.

But I think, finally, that the true greatness of this book is how, in giving her mother to us, Brown also keeps her for herself. In "In Memoriam" you have to read a footnote to find out the man Tennyson mourns was named Arthur Hallam, nor does Milton ever name Edward King in "Lycidas." The conventions of the pastoral led Milton to write one of the greatest poems of all time, but only at the loss of someone he'd loved very dearly. By contrast, Brown seems to slip into the conventions of the prose elegy as if into a borrowed jacket and make it her own, rather than getting lost inside it. This is practically literalized in a scene that takes places after Barbara Brown's body has been delivered to the crematorium.

> After a while I said, "Let's go up to the Ruins." They were these old cliff dwellings my mother had loved. We hadn't brought any of our hiking stuff down with us so we put on sweaters and coats and scarves of my mother's. We packed some picnic stuff and drove a couple hours into the mountains. We drove her car.
>
> There was snow on the side of the roads and some places on the road where the sun hadn't reached. The sky was clear and blue and the air was cold. I wore my mother's driving gloves as I drove. I put on her winter jacket when I got there.
>
> I'd been there lots before with her. It was one of her favorite places.

Here is a classic trope of the narrative elegy: the post-death action that seems slightly quirky—an archaeological expedition twelve hours after your mother's death?—until you realize it has something to do with the dead person: "I'd been there lots before with her." But it's important to remember this isn't merely a trope: it's something that actually happens. After spending months or years nursing someone, death steals not only one's parent and one's patient but also one's routine, and it can take a while to find activities to fill that void. While transitioning into a new phase, the caregiver often does things she once did with the dead person, or communes with mementos of the deceased's life. But Brown's choice of memento—"sweaters and coats and scarves of my mother's"—and the way she puts them to practical use speak to the very scene she's trying to find a way to describe in words. The slight awkwardness of wearing her mother's clothes is acknowledged by the way she lists first the items ("sweaters and coats and scarves") and then adds "of my mother's." But she doesn't let that stop her from using them for what she needs them to do: she needs something to keep her warm. What she doesn't need to do is go on the trip in the first place. *Excerpts*, you could argue, is as unnecessary as that trip to the Ruins, but that doesn't mean it's not valuable; and the use of convention in *Excerpts* is just like the use of Barbara Brown's clothing: borrowed, but entirely functional. Rebecca Brown relaxes into literary tradition, letting it gently shape every chapter, every scene, yet never letting it guide her toward a sentiment that, however grand or even true, would eclipse the woman who produced it. The "sweaters and coats and scarves" do not lead to some false sense of womblike closeness with her mother; indeed, the only way we know they keep Rebecca warm is because she doesn't say she's cold. Similarly, the cliff dwellings don't produce epiphanies of the enduring human spirit. All they do is remind a daughter of the mother she's lost:

> The year before she got sick, my mother had done volunteer
> work with an archaeology crew at a different Mogollon site.
> She learned, she told me, that the only remains these people
> left were some tools, some pieces of broken pottery and
> these ruins.

The temptation to add a final lofty sentiment to these two
sentences—some grand epiphany that would make a perma-
nent monument of her mother's life—must have been enormous, but Brown resists it, and it's this fortitude, this continual
choice of life over art, that awes and inspires me as both reader
and fellow writer.

In May 2003, Brown published a miscellany of autobiographical essays entitled *The End of Youth*, which dealt largely
with her father's death. The truly fragmentary nature of the
collection (as opposed to *Excerpts'* cohesive collage) reflects
Brown's relationship with her father in both life and death: he'd
already been gone for decades—he left the family when Rebecca was a teenager—and when he did die it was suddenly,
from a heart attack just a few weeks after her mother died of
cancer. In several of the pieces, one can see the biographical
sources of some of her novels, *The Children's Crusade* and *The
Haunted House* especially, and at the risk of being simplistic, one
wants to characterize these as Brown's paternal books. Like
her first two novels, *The End of Youth* concludes with a sense of
dissolution—nothing as dramatic as the surreal horrors that
fill her fiction, but a very real sense of being orphaned out of
one's childhood. By contrast, *Excerpts* (which was actually
written before most of the pieces in *The End of Youth*) renders
the horrors of cancer as fully as the tortures in novels like *The

Terrible Girls and *The Dogs*, but there is a confidence as well, both in Brown's voice and in her demeanor while she takes care of her mother. This is a liminal experience that Brown knows she will survive, even if her mother will not. This realization is never mentioned as such. It is instead taken for granted—is in some way irrelevant to the writer, whose gaze rests unblinkingly on her mother throughout the experience. The failure—or, more accurately, refusal—to produce a universal epiphany produces a much quieter realization, reminding us that consciousness, that identity itself, stands distinct from the cultural forces which, though they may allow us to measure it, never really allow us to see it.

Which leads me back to Brown's conceit. At first I thought it was simply extraneous, perhaps even (it is a strange word to use in the context of so rigorously plain a writer) fancy. *Excerpts From a Family Medical Dictionary.* But in fact there is no excerpting as such. Truncation yes, but the story that *is* here proceeds in a coherently linear fashion, as dying (as indeed life) always does. It was only as I approached the end of the book that I realized the concept of "excerpts" was less a narrative trope than a thematic one. Take, for example, the chapter entitled "Unction," which opens with the words "the act of anointing, as in medical treatment or a religious ceremony." The sterile definition stands in contrast to what follows:

We took turns holding the bowl and took turns washing.

Her body was hairless as a girl and it was smaller. She'd lost so much weight and her skin was loose, but when we washed her, lifting her hand, her arm, her foot, her neck, she gave to us. The tension in her body, how it was stiff and

clenched and could not bend or be turned easily the last days
of her life, the twitching and the rigidness her body had had
for days, had been released.

As the memoir progresses toward its inevitable conclusion, the
contrast between these brief introductory passages and what
actually happened reveals an ever-increasing intellectual and
emotional distance between lived experience and the words we
use to describe it. Brown's words profess no greater accuracy
than the scientific term at the head of each of her chapters; but
instead, by approaching the experience from a different tack,
they allow us to triangulate our position relative to the thing
which is lost.

Or maybe I'm dressing it up a bit. Maybe all these excerpts
do is save the writer—who is, after all, also a daughter—from
having to begin each chapter with the words she finally says on
page 84: "She's dead." What I mean is, maybe the conceit is less
thematic than psychological in nature; as Brown writes in a
slightly different context: "None of the drugs were to cure anymore. They were only to comfort." But Brown's technical in-
ventiveness has always been coupled with an entropic tendency
toward decay, by which I mean that she never erects an aesthetic edifice without tearing it down in the same book. The
paternal books end with the dissolution not only of the protagonist's identity (i.e., character), but with the traditional tools
by which identity is usually quantified, space and time (i.e., narrative); you have no idea whether you're inside the protagonists' heads or in the real world, but in either case you know it's
a really, *really* bad place. In the maternal books, by contrast,
Brown allows for the glimmer of some kind of rebirth or re-

building. The protagonists still go through hell, but in the end these ordeals seem cleansing, clarifying, if only in the sense that they destroy everything that had been there before and so make a fresh start possible. Indeed, reading through her previous nine books over the course of several months, I felt a bit like Dante being led through the various levels of hell. And, like Dante, I sometimes doubted my guide; but in the end she got me out alive.

Which leads me, somewhat abruptly (for some reason the end of an essay, no matter how overdue, often seems abrupt to me), back to my opening image: that coyote den, and the idea of liminality it represented. I want to embrace that image, but also let it go. Because when I think about it in the context of Rebecca Brown's work—when I think of it as a symbol *for* that work—I find myself inspired to feats of exegetical interpretation. The den's central strut becomes a brick of earth folded around open air like a sod mandorla. Or a cannoli shell from which the icing has been carefully licked, or a handle that God, if indeed he is made in our image, could slip a finger into and hurtle the planet along a cosmic alley like a galactic bowling ball. But at a certain point all this exegesis starts to feel a lot like digging: the more I take out, the bigger my hole gets. Eventually one has to stop digging, and take shelter.

Afterword: Stepford Novels, Henpecking, *Ulysses,* and a Note on the Title

Several years ago the *Village Voice* asked me to review a novel, the second book from a writer with a convincingly authorial pedigree. The novel is somewhat hard to categorize: it's an epistolary romance of sorts, sort of, which is to say that there aren't really letters and there isn't really romance either, but a man and a woman do interact through written media, and this correspondence eventually produces a sort of emotional and sexual *frisson*. The man and the woman meet electronically; hence the ontological and epistemological uncertainty over genre, labels, names. Their creator seems down with the particular line of thinking that posits the Internet as an unstable category of communication—a theory I find a little fancy myself—and the case could be made that on a mimetic level her book captures the banality inherent to the antihierarchical parentheses-within-parentheses presentation of information via email and chat rooms and bulletin boards. One could also argue, less charitably but more accurately, that in dutifully recording so many quotidian observations this novelist succeeds at little more than being quotidian.

But to dwell on this or any other subjective aspect of the book in question would be to miss the larger point: this novel's true act of mimesis isn't its imitation of e-speak, but rather its imitation of fiction. Its words describe "characters"; its characters have detailed "histories"; these histories grow sedimentarily into "narrative"; but calling that narrative a "novel" is akin to calling a pan of flour and water, dutifully mixed together and baked, "bread." The ingredients are there, but the flavor and style, the yeast and salt of art, are not. The book lacks neither coherence nor intelligence. What it lacks is imagination, linguistic flair, a raison d'être more compelling than its author's presumably well-intentioned intention to write, and as a result the final product proves nothing more than the execution of its premise, as fully explicated in the single paragraph of jacket copy as it is in 320 prettily packaged pages. Its destiny, I'm sure, is to take up space on the particle-board shelving units of the nation's chain bookstores, sandwiched in with the mass-produced simulacra that passes for literary fiction in America. Because, even allowing for the fact that any living literary community produces its fair share of James Fenimore Coopers and Pearl S. Bucks and Henry Millers and that it takes time to separate the chaff from the wheat; even taking into consideration the theory that cinematic and virtual media have displaced the printed word as the dominant narrative form and that the novel and its grown-too-big-for-its-britches sibling, the memoir, are only occasionally profitable anachronisms; even recognizing that literacy standards and technological advances have made it theoretically feasible for just about anyone to write and publish a book—even considering all these factors, the number of Stepford novels that are written, published, reviewed, and read every year is completely out of control. I'm not sure if it's because the standards for literary fiction have become so lax or simply because the conventions are so inbred, but it seems that anyone can write a novel these days. Not a mystery or a thriller or a romance or any other type of acknowledged formula fiction, but a *novel* (file under: Literature; see also: Classics).

Don't get me wrong. I'm not blaming this particular novelist for the phenomenon. Certainly I'd rather be writing novels than working in an office any day, and if she can pull it off then it's no one's fault but the people who pay her. Rather, blame Thomas More for writing *Utopia*. Blame Sartre for writing "The Wall," Doris Lessing for writing *The Golden Notebook*, Gore Vidal for writing all those historical diatribes, blame Don DeLillo just for writing (and Jonathan Franzen, God help us, for reading him). Blame the people who publish these books; blame the people who buy them. Blame the writing programs and the prize committees, blame the deconstructionist literary critics or the back-patting Siamese-twinned professions of writing and reviewing fiction, blame any or all of the identity communities who read and write those ethnic- or gender-marketed booster books or blame the dead white European males who forced us to resort to Literature as our Daily Affirmation in the first place. Blame whomever you want—but it seems to me that to summarize and evaluate yet another of these shadow fictions is to miss the point. These novels aren't *bad*. They just aren't novels. They aren't art. Real fiction doesn't "discover" truth, let alone present it to readers (that's why it's called fiction, duh): real fiction invents and dispenses with truth as it sees fit. That's why it's called *fiction*. Duh.

The writers reviewed in this book aren't Stepford novelists, with the exception of Jim Crace—but I had to read three or four of Crace's books to figure out what a Stepford novelist was—and Stanley Crouch, who, though a terrible novelist, is a gifted polemical essayist if also, unfortunately, a demagogue. But that's the kind of fickle reader I am: charitable to hopeless cases and harsh on writers with an authentic gift but, more than anything else, personally, *emotionally* involved in what I read. When I think a book has let me down I get angry with it, and when I think that book has deceived me I get pissed off. Thus my sharpest barbs and most inhospitable *ad hominems* tend to be directed at writers I genuinely admire, or in whom I see genuine, wasted talent. This is because I think of myself as a kind of mother hen, not so much of writers, but of the novel itself. Fiction is like dance: it's susceptible to the egos of its practitioners. Bad writers can't do it much damage because they'll simply be ignored, but a self-indulgent writer with a single compelling skill can do incalculable harm.

One of the most common criticisms I've received for these essays, especially from friends, is that I don't say much about the strengths of the writers I review. And it's true, I don't. Most of the novelists discussed in this collection had thousands of words devoted to their individual strengths long before I got around to cataloging their weaknesses: they don't need me to point them out again. And God knows I've never aspired to anything like impartiality. If anything, I've always considered my flagrant bias to be one of the saving graces of my reviews. If they're extreme in their opinions, that stridency can always be attributed to its author rather than to some kind of universal authority. The very extremity of my views does as much to undermine my authority as to enforce it, or at least I hope it does, because I am by no means convinced of the hallowedness of my own ideas. And talent, as I said earlier, isn't the issue here: content is, and context. It seems to me that there are two strains of literature currently in vogue—what I have referred to, for lack of more authoritative terms, as recherché postmodernism and recidivist realism—and both of them, in my opinion, suck. I'm not interested in pointing out how an author works well in one mode or another, or executes one aspect of one or another mode with a greater or lesser degree of success, because I think the modes need to be thrown out entirely. Not as tools for a writer sitting down to a blank page, but rather as the two poles they feel they must choose between, and against which they are judged.

The other thing I hear a lot is that I don't offer an alternative to the writing I spend so much time panning. If this is what writers shouldn't be doing, then what *should* they do? My feeling here is that the last thing readers need is a writer telling them what to read (besides his or her own books, of course). And as for writers: well, if you need me to tell you how to write a novel then you probably shouldn't be writing one in the first place. Nevertheless, there *are* some things I'd like to say to my peers. Still, it's hard to tell someone whom you admire (or respect, or want to help, or in some way engage with) that you think there are problems with his or her work, let alone that it's, well, *worthless*. These reviews, if not as direct as a coffee klatch (or barroom brawl), are, I hope, some kind of dialogue with my generation. If, in the end, I offer nothing more than a series of prohibitions, it's because I think it's precisely the need to sign on to a program that kills literature. As soon as a writer starts writing to belong to a tradition or a program or a school rather than to describe what's wrong with the world, he or she has gone from being, in the most hackneyed terms, part of the solution to part of the problem. Something which can be held up to a predetermined list of attributes that can be checked off one by one, so that a score of 80% makes it good, 90% makes it great, and 100% gets it a gold star, isn't art. It's high school— and bad high school at that. The year I graduated the valedictorian was well-known to be the best cheater in school: I helped him in English, my best friend let him look over his shoulder in math, and the science whiz (daughter of the science teacher no less) helped him with his experiments in biology and chemistry. As it happens he was not a particularly stupid guy, and he was also reasonably nice, which was probably why we all helped him. But we were all shocked—not to mention a little pissed off—when he got to give the commencement speech instead of one of us. I have no interest in contributing to another Cy Diller.

As one reads contemporary novelists, one can't shake the feeling that they write for one another rather than some more or less common reader. Their prose shares a showiness that speaks of solidarity and competition—the exaggerated panache with which teenaged boys shoot hoops in their driveway while pretending they don't know their neighbor is watching from across the street. Their individuality is lost inside this prose, again, like schoolboys lost inside a uniform of hoodies and fifties and baseball caps worn slightly askew—not, you know, sideways, like *black* people, just a little off center to show that they're down with it. *Word*. My hatred of all this teenaged posing has reached such a fever pitch that I'm willing to be clownish in my denunciation of it—to spew obscenities in ostensibly literary contexts or pose with an ax on the cover of this book. The plain truth is that I am less and less capable of intellectual engagement with contemporary fiction because I feel like I've been had when I do so: the very process of literary analysis legitimizes a body of work that I feel is simply unworthy of such attention. My generation has inherited a tradition that has grown increasingly esoteric and exclusionary, falsely intellectual and alienating to the mass of readers, and just as falsely comforting to those in the club. In place of centuries of straightforward class discrimination, the twentieth century invented an elitist rhetoric intelligible to only the most diligent and educated of readers—a club that doesn't exclude anyone per se, but makes you work very, very hard to join. In the process they lost not just the eye but the respect of a more general reading public, a respect that every generation since modernism has striven for unsuccessfully, trying to entice the common reader back into the fold with delicately carved morsels of rotting flesh they try to pass off as prime rib.

I will say it once and for all, straight out: it all went wrong with Joyce. *A Portrait of the Artist as a Young Man* is less a *bildungsroman* than the chapter by chapter unraveling of a talent which, if "The Dead" is any indication, could have been formidable, while *Ulysses* is nothing more than a hoax upon literature, a joint shenanigan of the author and the critical establishment predicated on two admirable, even beautiful fal-

lacies that were hopelessly contingent upon the historical circumstances which produced them: William James' late Victorian metaphor of the stream of consciousness, which today
seems closer to phrenology than modern notions of psychology and neurology; and T.S. Eliot's early modern fantasy of a
textual stockpile of intellectual history that would form an
allusive network of bridges to the cultural triumphs of the
ages, a Venice without the smell of sewage, or mustard gas.
Stein had done a beautiful duet with James' ideas in *Three Lives*
and other books, and Eliot was his own best pupil, but Stein,
for all her public boasting, was modest in her books, and Eliot
was also his own best critic—if not simply the best poet of
the twentieth century. It took an imagination as literal as
Joyce's, a temperament as dogged, an ambition as lacking
in nuance, to turn a book as lively as *The Odyssey* into a stale
monument to everything that had so recently failed the world.
That the book was so enthusiastically embraced represents less
a return to the right path that so many wishful readers—
including, at one point, Virginia Woolf—hoped it would be,
but rather a willful assumption of blinkers to the ways in which
a blending of the storied and historical notions of progress
had led the world so recently astray. For Joyce was not quite
a modernist and then again not quite a lapsed Catholic. He
lacked the doubt in language's ability to render the world that
had made the stream of consciousness so attractive to early
twentieth-century writers in the first place, but thought instead that he was producing a mimetic account of how the mind
worked; all you need then do is render a great mind—a mind
as great as, say, Joyce's—and your problems would melt
away. And yes, Joyce, like the other writers I've written about

here, has his strengths; but it is his failings that have been most successful, most pervasive in their effect. *Ulysses* has served since its publication as the ideal for serious writers, and the twentieth century is littered with magnum opuses that have been written under its sway, and that have marked the nadir of their various writers' careers.

If you aren't a novelist, I'm not sure you can imagine what it feels like to write such heresy. Though I normally write in the morning, I am writing this in the middle of the night like a fugitive; my hands are literally shaking as I type. Sometimes even I am overwhelmed by the extent of the reevaluation I'm calling for, the sheer fucking presumptuousness of it. The excision from the canon, or at least the demotion in status, of most of Joyce, half of Faulkner and Nabokov, nearly all of Gaddis, Pynchon, DeLillo, not to mention the general dumping of their contemporary heirs. And then there's that other strain, which I can hardly bear to slog through, the realists and the realists and the *realists*, too many to name, too many to contemplate really, their rational, utilitarian platitudes rolling out endlessly like toilet paper off a spindle. Even I ask myself who in the hell I am to say these things. But a piecemeal approach won't do anymore. The problem is too widespread within the insular literary and publishing world to merely pick at its edges: the entire scab must be ripped off.

Learning to like experimental literature was, for most readers, a monumental task, unlearning it positively Sisyphean. It's not hard for me to find people who agree with me about one or two of the writers I've reviewed—this person dislikes Moody, that person can't stand Wallace, another just doesn't get Whitehead. But dissing them all? And the people who produced them? Eyes glaze over, tongues get tangled. Yet almost anyone will admit that literature is an inherited form, that each new generation learns from its predecessors. If we can accept that we build on our predecessors' strengths, then why can't we accept that we might build on their mistakes as well? Wasn't that, after all, the premise of the modernist revolution? That thirty centuries of Western culture had led not to a pinnacle of achievement but instead to the industrialized, assembly-line slaughter of soldiers and civilians in World War I? Certainly the postmodernists thought so when it happened again a quarter century later, with concentration camps thrown in as a *coup de grace*.

Why is it so hard to think that a literary program forged under duress should have at its heart a fatal flaw? That, looking back, the first and second world wars seem less and less like aberrations and more and more like periodic irruptions that are as much a part of our way of life as inflation and unemployment are parts of capitalist cycles? And that now might be a good time to try to decide on a different strategy, when the entire world, as fucked up as it might be, is not fucked up the way it was then? Because make no mistake: every writer wants to save the world. Or, more accurately, art, like political activism, seeks to make itself unnecessary. Embedded in every story, every poem, every play is a utopian vision that, if achieved, would make the words irrelevant, redundant, unnecessary. Parody and pastiche have run their course in that effort. Their mockery does little more than affirm the power of the thing mocked. It's high time for a literature that opts out of such a limited, dysphonic call-and-response paradigm, and instead offers a real alternative, an imaginative solution that hints at some-

thing beyond the juvenile culture that today's writers spend so
much time making fun of in such a jejune manner. Isn't that a
more worthwhile goal for a generation of writers to work toward, rather than toward their own fame?

And so my title: *Hatchet Jobs*. What I wanted to suggest is
not so much the negative aspect of these essays, which will be
pretty obvious to anyone who can read, but rather my own
metaphor for the process which came to dominate my thinking
as I shaped this book. My goal was never to offer an alternative
model to the kinds of writing I discuss here, because it's precisely when a line is drawn in the sand that people begin to toe
it and you fall into the trap of reification, of contemporaneity,
an inability to react to changing circumstances. Rather than
make my own claims as to what fiction should be—claims
which I make all the time, and which primarily have to do with
the work of an individual writer, usually me—I wanted only to
hack away the dead wood in order to discover the heart of the
novel. That heart is, I believe, still beating, is still strong and
vital, and needs no help of mine to grow, but only to be seen. Of
course the heart in question isn't a heart, but rather a diffuse
locus of ideas and ideologies loosely tethered to a set of individual visions and personalities. None is complete in itself—
there is no Borgesian aleph hidden from view, no new *Ulysses*
waiting to be written or third party to fall between the late
postmodernists and recidivist realists—but rather a true republic of literature composed of single votes in the form of single writers, even single books. If I rarely point them out
directly, it's because a book should be discovered on its own
terms—or on the reader's—but never on the critic's. For the
same reasons that I feel I have been effectively silenced by

being labeled a bitch, or that Kurt Vonnegut has been silenced by being deified, I am leery of telling people what to look for, lest that's precisely what they find.

If you remember one thing about these essays, remember that a novelist wrote them, not a critic, and that novelists lie for a living. Before there is fiction's much-vaunted truth, there is the lie—the invention, fabrication, prevarication, the *fiction*. That lie is the engine of history, of love and capital and science. The poet's dream is a carrot we all chase at one time or another—and yeah, history *is* a story, at least the way we tell it. Setup, rising action, climax, dénouement. The basic elements are borrowed from fiction in a chronological syntax as rigid as grammar itself. But chronology's just a mental conceit imitating time, linearity a narrative conceit imitating chronology. It's all metaphor, and metaphor is language's mercenary: it'll work for anyone. That novelists have dragged metaphor into service as their primary foot soldier reflects my own experience of literature, which is that it's first and foremost an attack on life, sometimes overtly, but more often hiding the truth from itself (anger and denial, Kübler-Ross' first two stages of grief). Literature is an act of revenge that aspires to elegy. It mourns what it isn't—what it thinks it has killed by comparison. Semiotically, syntactically: at the level of the sign and the level of the sentence, from which all narrative proceeds, language waters the seeds of its own failure. Not just its inability to *be* what it *names*, but the immense difficulty of measuring the gap between. Of distance? Of closeness? It depends on whether you see the cup as half full or half empty. But it's only after a work of literature has accepted its own failure—has, as it were, elegized its stillborn self—that it can begin the complex series of contextual manipulations by which meaning is created and we locate ourselves as surely as the ancient navigators fixed their positions between stars. In recent years we have been far, far too busy celebrating our Pyrrhic victories to examine our much greater failures. Contemporary novels have either counterfeited reality, or forfeited it. In their stead we need a new materialism.